Mary Berry is known to millions through her regular cookery spot on Thames Television's magazine programme, *After Noon Plus*. She is a regular contributor to BBC *Woman's Hour* and often takes part in BBC and local radio phone-in programmes.

Mary Berry was, for several years, cookery editor of *Ideal Home* and is now the *Home and Freezer Digest*'s cookery consultant. She is one of Britain's most popular cookery writers and has written over twenty cookery books.

*Also by Mary Berry in Sphere Books:*

FAST CAKES

# Fruit Fare

**MARY BERRY**

SPHERE BOOKS LIMITED
30 32 Gray's Inn Road, London WC1X 8JL

First published in Great Britain by
Judy Piatkus (Publishers) Ltd 1982
Copyright © Mary Berry 1982
Published by Sphere Books Ltd 1983

TRADE
MARK

Set in Zapf

Reproduced, printed and bound in Great Britain by
Hazell Watson & Viney Ltd, Aylesbury, Bucks

A big thank you to Clare Blunt for her meticulous help in recipe development and testing. Between us we have five children – Timothy, Kate, Thomas, William and Annabel – and I should like to thank them for being such avid tasters.

# Contents

# Introduction

Fruit is everywhere: in High Street supermarkets, in top people's grocers, on market stalls, on trees in country gardens, on barrows at street corners. Gleaming oranges, shining apples, hothouse grapes, peaches, plums, melons, strawberries in season – wherever you go, people are buying fruit, growing it, eating it. Never before has fruit been so popular.

It comes to us from all over the world as well as from our own back gardens, from the fruit farms and orchards of England and Scotland and from the orange groves of the warm Mediterranean countries. Swift modern transport, combined with advanced methods of refrigeration, brings fresh fruit from the tropics to our tables all the year round and the modern housewife takes it for granted that she can go and buy a lemon any time she wants one. We are now, in Britain, becoming familiar with exotic fruit that we had only read about a generation ago.

Our own fruit, thanks to modern methods of cultivation, grows bigger and better and there is more of it. Even the soft fruits of summer extend their season well into the autumn. More and more new varieties come on to the market and their uses are innumerable. For dessert fruit you will choose the best, sweetest and juiciest; but smaller specimens can be used for cooking, jam or marmalade making, for chutneys, sauces and preserves. There are canned and dried fruits too.

Probably the biggest revolution in our kitchens has been the domestic freezer. Using it to its best advantage, you can be sure of a supply of your favourite fruits throughout the year. While fresh fruit for eating immediately should be bought in small quantities and used at once, the amount of frozen fruit you can have on hand depends only on the amount your freezer will hold. In most cases it will keep very well for up to a year, so that you can have, for instance, frozen raspberries from one season to the next. A big advantage is that you can buy fruit when it is plentiful and cheap – or harvest your own – and freeze it for the rest of the year. However, only fruit of the best quality should be deep frozen. Never freeze raw fruit that is over-ripe and mushy, or has been damaged or blemished.

There are four main methods of freezing fruit. In dry freezing, which is suitable for most of the berries, the fruit is spread out on trays, frozen quickly and then packed in polythene containers. In dry sugar packing (for melon, citrus fruits, pineapple) the fruit is layered with sugar in polythene bags or containers and frozen. In a syrup pack (for stone fruits, apples, pears and melons) it is covered with syrup in the container. Finally the fruit can be puréed, either cooked (apples, plums, damsons) or uncooked (strawberries, raspberries, peaches) depending on the type. The purée is then frozen and is particularly useful for fools, sauces and sorbets.

You can freeze and store nuts for long periods. Don't forget that they are fruits too! I have nuts in my freezer in individual small polythene bags, which are packed inside another big polythene bag to keep them together. They have been there for years and are still perfect.

# Apple

As children we ducked for apples at Hallowe'en, in a big tub of water surrounded by towels to protect the floor. It was a moment of triumph when you emerged, water up your nose and the apple stalk firmly between your teeth. There was something magic about apples at that time of year. Then there were the toffee apples at summer fairs, with their gleaming, brittle, amber-coloured coating hiding the juicy fruit inside.

The apple is the universally beloved fruit. Eat it raw, polished and crisp, eat it with cheese. Bake it in a pie, use it as a sauce or as a drink. Enjoy it.

Apple trees flourish all over the temperate regions of the world, and nowhere better than in the British Isles. In fact, a good apple year in the south of England can be positively embarrassing to the owner of a few trees, who simply cannot give the fruit away.

Apples today are in the shops all the year round, thanks to modern methods of transport, storage and refrigeration. The main producing countries are Britain, France, the United States, Canada, Australia, New Zealand and South Africa. In the Northern Hemisphere the season runs from August to March, in the Southern from March to September.

Apples divide into dessert (or eating) and cooking varieties. Keep the cooking ones strictly for the kitchen, but eaters, if they are firm enough, will cook perfectly well when required.

Think of cooking apples and you usually think of Bramley Seedling, which is large and well-flavoured and bakes beautifully – ideal for pies. But there are many others that have stood the test of time, almost all of them native to Britain – for instance Grenadier, Lord Derby, Newton Wonder, Early Victory. Similarly among dessert apples Cox's Orange Pippin reigns supreme in England. But try Laxton's Superb, James Grieve, Elliston's Orange – all of them English grown. Among the imports are Golden Delicious, Granny Smith, Dunn's Seedling, Red Delicious and Jonathan.

Apples are best eaten fresh, so do not buy too many at a time.

Choose good firm-looking fruit, avoiding any that are bruised or showing signs of decay at the core ends. Apples past their prime look lustreless and the flesh will be soft and tasteless. When storing large quantities at home – perhaps from your own trees – pack them in well-ventilated boxes. Do not let the fruit touch each other and keep the boxes in a cool place. Examine them regularly for signs of decay and remove any affected fruit before it can spoil the rest.

Apples may be frozen either peeled, sliced and blanched without sugar, or cooked with sugar. Cook with sugar for pies and puddings, or purée for sauce and baby food. They should keep for one year or until the next crop is ready. It goes without saying that you should freeze only the best quality fruit – this applies to *all* fruit.

# Curried Apple Soup

Serves 6

*Fruit soups are rather unusual but they can taste quite delicious.*

1 oz (25 g) butter
1 onion, finely chopped
1½ oz (40 g) flour
1 level tablespoon curry powder
1½ pints (900 ml) water

2 chicken stock cubes
1½ lb (675 g) cooking apples, peeled, cored and roughly chopped
juice of half a lemon
salt and pepper
¼ pint (150 ml) single cream

Melt the butter in a large saucepan, add the onion and fry slowly, with the lid on, for 10 minutes or until soft.

Stir in the flour and curry powder and cook for 1 minute. Add water, stock cubes, apples and lemon juice and bring to the boil, stirring continually, and simmer for 15 minutes. Leave the soup to cool slightly and then sieve or purée in a blender.

Rinse out the saucepan, return the soup to the saucepan and bring to the boil. Taste and check seasoning. If necessary, add a little extra stock to thin down the soup.

Pour a little cream on top of each bowl of soup as it is served.

# Bacon and Apple Turnover

Serves 4 to 6

*This is a good way of using up the last few slices of a boiled bacon joint.*

12 oz (350 g) cooked bacon or ham pieces
1 large cooking apple, peeled and cored
1 small onion

2 tablespoons stock
ground black pepper
8 oz (227 g) packet puff pastry
1 egg, beaten

Heat the oven to 425 °F, 220 °C, gas mark 7.

Mince the ham, apple and onion and put into a bowl. Stir in the stock, add a little freshly ground black pepper – usually no salt is needed.

Roll out the pastry to an oblong 14 by 10 inches (35 by 25 cm), brush the edges with a little beaten egg and place the ham filling in the centre. Fold over the pastry and firmly seal the edges. Trim and then place on a baking sheet and make three slits in the centre of the pastry. Brush over with beaten egg and bake in the oven for about 30 minutes until the pastry is crisp and golden brown.

Carefully lift onto a serving dish and serve with browned cauliflower cheese or cold with salads.

# Apple Whirligig
Serves 4

*A good pudding for a winter day. Instead of apples you could use gooseberries, plums or damsons. (Always use a dark-coloured jam.)*

| | |
|---|---|
| 1 lb (450 g) cooking apples | 4 oz (100 g) self-raising flour |
| 4 rounded tablespoons | 1 level tablespoon caster sugar |
|    well-flavoured red jam | 2 oz (50 g) margarine |
| 2 tablespoons water | about 3 tablespoons milk |

Heat the oven to 425 °F, 220 °C, gas mark 7.

Butter a shallow ovenproof dish. Peel, quarter, core and slice the apples and place them in the dish. Blend 2 tablespoons of the jam with the water and pour over the apples. Bake in the oven for 10 minutes.

Meanwhile, put the flour in a bowl with the sugar, add the margarine cut in small pieces. Rub in the margarine with your fingertips until the mixture resembles fine breadcrumbs. Add the milk and mix with a knife to make a firm dough.

Roll out on a floured surface to an oblong 8 by 6 inches (20 cm by 15 cm), spread with the remaining jam and then roll up, from the long side, like a Swiss roll and cut into 8 slices.

Take the dish from the oven and place the slices of dough around the edge of the dish, leaving a space between each. Return to the oven and bake for a further 15 minutes until the apple is tender and the scones risen and golden brown.

Serve hot with custard.

# Lamb and Apple Curry

Serves 4

*If you do not have as much as 12 oz (350 g) cold lamb, you can always use half as much and add a hard-boiled egg to each serving.*

1 oz (25 g) dripping
1 large onion, chopped
2 sticks celery, chopped
1 oz (25 g) flour
2 level teaspoons curry powder or to taste

¾ pint (450 ml) stock
2 cooking apples, peeled, cored and diced
12 oz (350 g) cold roast lamb
salt and pepper

Melt the dripping in a saucepan and add the onion and celery. Cook gently for 5 minutes, then stir in the flour and curry powder and cook for a further 2 to 3 minutes. Add the stock and bring to the boil, stirring until the sauce has thickened. Cover the pan and simmer gently for 20 minutes, then stir in the apples and continue cooking for another 10 minutes.

Add the meat, cut into neat pieces, and simmer for a further 10 minutes. Taste and check seasoning and serve with plain boiled rice and, if liked, side dishes of poppadums, chutney, sliced banana and peanuts.

# Red Cabbage and Apples

Serves 6 to 8

*This dish freezes and reheats exceptionally well. It goes very well with pork sausages or chops. Try it with the Sunday roast as a change.*

1 medium-sized red cabbage
1 lb (450 g) apples, weighed after peeling and coring
¼ pint (150 ml) cider or stock
1½ oz (40 g) sugar

1 level teaspoon salt
4 cloves
6 tablespoons vinegar
2 oz (50 g) butter
1 tablespoon red currant jelly

Trim, clean and finely shred the cabbage. Slice the apples and place with the cabbage in a saucepan. Add the cider, sugar, salt and cloves. Cover and simmer for about 45 minutes, until the apples are tender.

Remove the cloves and add the vinegar, butter and red currant jelly. Blend well over the heat, taste and check seasoning and serve hot.

## Cheese, Celery and Apple Salad                    Serves 4

*This salad is ideal for a vegetarian meal. Eat it with wholemeal bread rolls and butter for a satisfying and nutritious lunch.*

6 sticks celery, finely sliced
2 red eating apples, cored and
  diced
8 oz (225 g) blue cheese, cubed

4 tablespoons oil
1 tablespoon mayonnaise
salt and pepper to taste
lettuce and cucumber

Put the celery, apples and cheese in a bowl and stir lightly to mix.

Whisk together the oil, mayonnaise and seasoning, pour over the celery mixture and toss lightly.

Arrange a bed of lettuce on a serving dish and spoon the salad into the centre and garnish with slices of cucumber.

## Waldorf Salad                    Serves 4

*There is no need to peel the apples for this salad. The skins add a dash of colour.*

4 dessert apples
3 sticks celery
2 oz (50 g) walnuts
4 rounded tablespoons
  mayonnaise

4 tablespoons lightly whipped
  double cream
a little lemon juice
salt
freshly ground black pepper
lettuce leaves

Wipe the apples; quarter, core and slice and put in a bowl. Finely slice the celery, coarsely chop the nuts and add to the apples.

Blend the mayonnaise with the cream and lemon juice to taste, season well and stir into the apple mixture so as to coat the apple thoroughly in order that it will not discolour.

Cover the bowl and leave in a cool place for at least 1 hour for the flavours to blend.

When ready to serve, taste and check seasoning. Arrange a bed of lettuce leaves on a serving dish and spoon the salad into the centre.

# Cheese and Apple Rarebit                    Serves 4

*If you have no chives, use snipped green onion tops or spring onions.*

4 oz (100 g) Cheddar cheese, grated
1 medium-sized cooking apple, peeled and grated

1 tablespoon chives, finely chopped
about 1 rounded tablespoon mayonnaise
4 slices hot toast

Put the cheese, apple and chives in a bowl and mix together. Then add sufficient mayonnaise to bind.

Heat the grill to hot and place the slices of toast in the grill pan. Spoon the mixture on top and return to the grill for 2 to 3 minutes until the mixture is golden brown and bubbling. Serve the rarebit at once.

# Baked Apple Dumplings                    Serves 4

*If your family does not like the taste of ginger, try adding cinnamon or grated lemon to the sugar and raisin filling.*

10 oz (275 g) plain flour
2½ oz (62 g) margarine
2½ oz (62 g) lard
about 3 tablespoons cold water
4 medium-sized cooking apples, peeled and cored

1½ oz light soft brown sugar
1½ oz (40 g) raisins
pinch of ginger
milk

Heat the oven to 400°F, 200°C, gas mark 6.

Make the pastry as for Deep Apple Pie (see page 20) and divide into 4 equal pieces. Roll each piece into a 7 inch (17.5 cm) circle.

Put an apple into the centre of each pastry round. Mix the sugar, raisins and ginger together and use to fill the centre of each apple. Brush edges of pastry with milk and bring them together over the apples, trimming neatly if necessary, and pressing to a neat shape.

Put the apples on a lightly greased baking sheet with the sealed edge underneath. Make a hole in the centre top of each dumpling. Roll out any pastry trimmings and use to make leaves with which to decorate the dumplings.

Brush with milk and bake in the oven for 35 to 45 minutes until lightly browned.

Serve hot with custard.

# Roast Pork with Apple Stuffing

Serves 8

*Stuffed pork makes an excellent Sunday lunch. Breadcrumbs freeze well so when you come across an unappetising end of loaf, turn it into breadcrumbs. Keep these, for up to 3 months, in the freezer and use in stuffings and charlottes.*

3 lb (1.4 kg) piece spare rib of
    pork

*Stuffing:*

1½ oz (40 g) butter
1 onion, chopped
2 small sticks celery, finely
    sliced
1 cooking apple, peeled, cored
    and diced

3 oz (75 g) wholemeal
    breadcrumbs
1 egg, beaten
salt and pepper

Heat the oven to 350 °F, 180 °C, gas mark 4.

Lay the pork flat; if it has been rolled and tied up at the butchers, take off all the string and open it out.

Melt the butter for the stuffing in a small saucepan and then add the onion and celery. Cover the saucepan and cook gently for 10 minutes, then stir in the apple and cook for a further 2 minutes. Take the pan from the heat and stir in the breadcrumbs and beaten egg and then season to taste. Leave to cool.

Put the stuffing into the pork and press back into shape and tie up with fine string or secure with skewers.

Place the pork on a grid in the meat tin, brush with a little oil and then sprinkle with salt. Roast in the oven for about 2 hours 20 minutes or until the meat is tender and the juices run clear.

Serve with Cider Apple Sauce (see page 30).

# Apple Charlotte

Serves 4 to 6

*This is a good, old-fashioned pudding – and an ideal way to use up white bread which is no longer fresh.*

| | |
|---|---|
| 1½ lb (675 g) cooking apples | 1 egg, separated |
| 2 tablespoons water | 5 to 6 oz (150 to 175 g) butter |
| 4 oz (100 g) caster sugar | 6 to 7 slices white bread |

Peel, core and slice the apples and place them in a thick saucepan together with the water and sugar. Cover and cook very gently until soft and thick.

Remove from the heat and stir in the egg yolk. Beat well. Taste and add extra sugar if liked.

Heat the oven to 400 °F, 200 °C, gas mark 6.

Melt the butter in a saucepan and use some of it to brush over the sides of a 6 inch (15 cm) cake tin. Then sprinkle with a little caster sugar so that the tin is completely coated.

Remove the crusts from the bread, leave two slices whole and cut the remainder into 1½ inch (3.75 cm) wide strips. Dip both sides of the strips of bread in the melted butter and press into the tin around the sides, leaving no gaps. Cover the base with one large slice of bread dipped in butter.

Lightly beat the egg white and brush over the joints – this will help to strengthen them. Spoon in the apple purée. Dip the remaining slice of bread in the last of the butter and use to cover the top of the apple. If necessary, trim the strips of bread around the side of the charlotte so that they are level.

Bake in the oven for 20 minutes, then reduce the heat to 375 °F, 190 °C, gas mark 5 and bake for a further 40 minutes until the bread is golden brown and crisp.

Run a knife around the charlotte and then turn out on to a serving dish. Serve with cream.

# Caramel Apple Rings

Serves 4

*This is really a very easy pudding to make. You can use windfalls, although they will probably have to be cut into pieces rather than into rings.*

2 oz (50 g) butter — 4 medium-sized cooking apples
4 oz (100 g) demerara sugar

Melt the butter and demerara sugar in a frying pan, stirring gently to allow the sugar to dissolve.

Peel and core the apples and cut each into 3 to 4 rings. Put in the frying pan and cook through gently for 5 to 6 minutes, turning once.

Carefully lift the rings out and serve with the sauce spooned over and plenty of pouring cream.

# Apple Strudel

Serves 6

*Apple Strudel is not difficult to make and it is a good way to use up windfalls if you have them.*

2 pieces strudel pastry, each 16 inches (40 cm) square
1½ oz (40 g) butter, melted
2 oz (50 g) white breadcrumbs

*Filling:*
1½ lb (675 g) cooking apples peeled, cored and finely diced
3 oz (75 g) light soft brown or caster sugar
1 level teaspoon cinnamon
2 oz (50 g) sultanas
grated rind of 1 orange
2 oz (50 g) ground almonds

Heat the oven to 400 F, 200 °C, gas mark 6.

Lay the two pieces of strudel pastry flat on a clean surface, brush with melted butter and sprinkle with most of the breadcrumbs.

Mix all the filling ingredients together and divide between the two pieces of strudel pastry, leaving a ½ inch (1.25 cm) border. Fold in these borders and then carefully roll up the pastry like a Swiss roll.

Place the strudels on a baking sheet, brush each with more melted butter and sprinkle with the rest of the breadcrumbs.

Bake in the oven for 30 minutes, brushing once or twice with more melted butter, until golden brown.

Leave to cool on the baking sheet, then cut into slices and lift on to a serving dish.

If liked, sprinkle the apple strudels with a little sieved icing sugar before serving.

# Deep Apple Pie

*Bramleys are best for apple pie because they keep their shape. There is no need to use perfect apples; use up windfalls if you have them. You can turn the pie into a crumble by leaving out the water from the pastry ingredients, adding 2 oz (50 g) sugar, and sprinkling the mixture over the top of the apples.*

1½ lb (675 g) cooking apples
2 to 3 oz (50 to 75 g) caster
   sugar
4 cloves
3 tablespoons cold water

*Pastry:*
6 oz (175 g) plain flour
1½ oz (40 g) margarine
1½ oz (40 g) lard
about 6 teaspoons cold water
   to mix
milk to glaze
granulated sugar

Put a pie funnel in the centre of a 1½ pint (900 ml) pie dish. Peel and core the apples and cut into thick slices. Arrange half the slices in the bottom of the pie dish, sprinkle with sugar and strew the cloves evenly amongst the apple. Cover with the remaining apple slices and add about 3 tablespoons cold water.

Sift the flour into a bowl and add the fats, cut into small pieces. Rub in with the fingertips until the mixture resembles fine breadcrumbs, then add sufficient cold water to mix to a firm dough. Roll out the pastry on a floured surface and cover the top of the pie with it. Use any trimmings to decorate, if liked. Chill the pie in the refrigerator for 30 minutes.

Heat the oven to 400 °F, 200 °C, gas mark 6. Brush the pie with a little milk and sprinkle the top with granulated sugar; make a small slit in the centre for the steam to escape. Bake in the oven for 40 to 50 minutes until the apple is tender and the pastry crisp and golden brown.

# Apple and Blackberry Pie

Make as above, using quarter the amount of blackberries to apple.

# Mincemeat and Apple Tart

Serves 6 to 8

*Bought mincemeat tends to be very spicy and strongly flavoured and is, I think, greatly improved by adding apple. This also makes it go further.*

8 oz (225 g) strong plain flour
½ level teaspoon salt
6 oz (175 g) hard margarine,
  chilled
about 9 tablespoons cold water
  or a scant ¼ pint (150 ml)

1 lb (450 g) jar mincemeat
1 large cooking apple, peeled,
  cored and sliced
milk to glaze
caster sugar

Sift the flour and salt into a bowl. Coarsely grate the margarine into the bowl. Stir in just sufficient water to make a firm dough. Roll out on a lightly floured surface to make a strip about ½ inch (1.25 cm) thick and 6 inches (15 cm) wide. Fold the pastry in three and give it a quarter turn to the left. Roll out again into a strip and fold in three. Wrap the pastry in foil and chill in the refrigerator for 30 minutes.

Heat the oven to 425°F, 220°C, gas mark 7.

Divide the pastry into two portions, one slightly larger than the other. Roll out the smaller portion to ⅛ inch (3 mm) thick circle and use it to line an 8 inch (20 cm) pie plate made of enamel or tin. Spoon the mincemeat into the dish and cover with slices of apple.

Roll out the remaining pastry to a circle about ¼ inch (6 mm) thick. Brush the edges of the pastry already in the tin with milk and cover the filling with the second piece of pastry. Press the edges together to seal and then crimp to make a decorative finish. Chill in the refrigerator for 10 minutes.

Brush the top of the pie with a little milk and then bake in the oven for 35 minutes, or until the pastry is golden brown and well risen.

Sprinkle with sugar and serve warm.

# Apple and Orange Pudding

Serves 6

*This is a lovely, light pudding, but if you like a slightly sharper taste, use the rind and juice of a lemon instead of the orange.*

4 large cooking apples
grated rind and juice of 1 small
  orange
2½ oz (62 g) fresh white
  breadcrumbs

½ oz (12.5 g) butter, melted
3 oz (75 g) caster sugar
2 eggs, separated
3 tablespoons caster sugar

Heat the oven to 350 °F, 180 °C, gas mark 4. Thoroughly butter a 2½ pint (1.4 litre) ovenproof dish.

Peel and coarsely grate the apples into a large bowl. Stir in the orange rind and juice, breadcrumbs, butter, 3 oz (75 g) caster sugar and the egg yolks. Mix thoroughly.

In another bowl, whisk the egg whites until they are stiff. Whisk in the remaining 3 tablespoons caster sugar, a teaspoonful at a time. Whisk the meringue into the apple mixture and turn it at once into the buttered dish and bake in the oven for 50 to 60 minutes, until the pudding is pale golden brown and crisp on top and the apple is cooked.

Serve at once with a jug of pouring cream.

# Apple, Pear and Honey Pie

Serves 6

*Apple pies are always popular, and this recipe makes an excellent variation.*

**Pastry:**
6 oz (175 g) plain flour
1½ oz (40 g) lard
1½ oz (40 g) butter
2 to 3 tablespoons cold water

**Filling:**
1 lb (450 g) cooking apples
1 lb (450 g) pears
juice of half a lemon
4 tablespoons clear honey
milk or water to glaze
a little granulated sugar

Heat the oven to 400 °F, 200 °C, gas mark 6.

Measure the flour into a bowl. Add the fats, cut into small pieces, and rub them in until the mixture resembles fine breadcrumbs. Add sufficient water to mix to a firm dough. Leave to rest in a cool place while preparing the filling.

Peel, core and slice the apples and pears and place them in a large bowl, together with the lemon juice and honey. Stir carefully so that the fruit is evenly coated.

Turn the fruit into a 2 pint (a good litre) pie dish.

Roll out the pastry on a floured surface and then cover the top of the pie with it. Re-roll any trimmings and cut them into leaves and use for decoration.

Stand the pie on an ovenproof dish or tray. Brush the pastry with a little milk or water and sprinkle with granulated sugar. Make a small slit in the centre for the steam to escape.

Bake the pie in the oven for 40 to 45 minutes until the fruit is tender and the pastry crisp and golden brown.

Serve warm with cream.

# Eve's Pudding

Serves 6

*If you are making sponge cakes, make an Eve's Pudding at the same time; it uses the same mixture as a Victoria Sponge. You can vary the fruit; try plums, damsons, apricots, loganberries or add blackberries to the apple.*

1 lb (450 g) cooking apples,
  peeled, cored and sliced
3 oz (75 g) demerara sugar
grated rind and juice of 1 lemon
4 oz (100 g) soft margarine

4 oz (100 g) caster sugar
2 eggs
4 oz (100 g) self-raising flour
1 level teaspoon baking powder

Heat the oven to 350°F, 180°C, gas mark 4. Grease a 2 pint (1 litre) ovenproof dish and put in the apples. Sprinkle with demerara sugar and the lemon juice and rind.

Put the margarine, caster sugar, eggs, flour and baking powder in a bowl and beat well for a minute until well blended. Spread the mixture over the apples and bake in the centre of the oven for about 1 hour. Test by pressing with a finger; if done the sponge will spring back when lightly touched.

Serve hot with custard.

# Baked Apples                                    Serves 4

*No pudding could be easier! You only need large, fat, unblemished apples; the filling can be concocted from anything you have to hand. Try honey or golden syrup; chopped almonds and dried fruit; apricot jam and dates; or lemon curd and chopped dried figs.*

4 large cooking apples          2 tablespoons water
mincemeat

Heat the oven to 350 °F, 180 °C, gas mark 4.
   Wipe the apples and remove the cores, using a sharp knife or corer, and make a slit around the centre of each apple.
   Place the apples in an ovenproof dish. Fill the centres with mincemeat and place a knob of butter on top of each apple.
   Pour the water around and then bake in the oven for 40 to 45 minutes until the apples are puffy and soft.
   Serve hot with thick cream or ice cream.

# Apple Cinnamon Shortcake                        Serves 6

*A great favourite – and this recipe can also be made with strawberries or raspberries. Bake the two rounds of shortcake separately on a baking sheet for about 20 minutes until they are a very pale golden brown. Cool and then fill with sliced strawberries or raspberries and whipped cream. Omit the cinnamon.*

6 oz (175 g) self-raising flour     half an egg, beaten
1 level teaspoon cinnamon           6 oz (175 g) apples, peeled,
4 oz (100 g) butter                    cored and sliced
3 oz (75 g) caster sugar            1 tablespoon demerara sugar

Heat the oven to 375 °F, 190 °C, gas mark 5. Grease a 7 inch (17.5 cm) square tin.
   Sift the flour and cinnamon into a bowl and rub in the butter until the mixture resembles fine breadcrumbs. Add the caster sugar and beaten egg and knead together. Turn on to a floured surface and knead lightly until smooth.
   Either press out the mixture lightly with the fingertips or use a

rolling pin to roll it gently to the correct size. Spread half over the base of the tin, arrange the apples neatly over it and then cover with the remaining piece of shortbread. Sprinkle with demerara sugar.

Bake in the oven for 45 minutes until the apple is cooked through and the topping a pale golden brown. Remove from the oven and allow to cool slightly. Serve warm with cream.

## Apple and Cinnamon Pancakes
Makes 8 to 10 pancakes

*An excellent pudding for children and adults alike.*

8 to 10 pancakes (see Crêpes
Suzette, page 121).

*Filling:*
4 large Bramley apples, peeled,
cored and sliced

¼ teaspoon ground cinnamon
6 oz (175 g) demerara sugar
4 oz (100 g) butter
sugar

Make the pancakes and put them on one side.

Put the apples in a saucepan and cook them gently with the cinnamon, sugar and 2 oz (50 g) butter, stirring occasionally, for about 20 minutes or until the apples are tender and the mixture is a thick pulp.

Spread out the pancakes on a flat surface. Divide the apple filling between them and roll up.

Melt the remaining butter in a frying pan and fry the rolled-up pancakes on all sides until they are brown. Transfer them to a warm serving dish and sprinkle with a little extra sugar and more ground cinnamon.

Serve hot with cream or ice cream.

## Blackberry and Apple Pancakes
Makes 8 to 10 pancakes

Use 1 lb (450 g) cooking apples, 8 oz (225 g) blackberries and 4 oz (100 g) granulated sugar and prepare the filling as above. Mix 1 level tablespoon cornflour with 1 tablespoon water, add to the fruit pulp and stir continually over the heat until the mixture thickens.

Fill the pancakes, fry and serve sprinkled with granulated sugar.

# Fruit Fritters

Serves 4

*Sometimes I make Fruit Fritters for a children's tea, particularly when I have an abundance of apples.*

1 lb (450 g) cooking apples, or bananas or apricots or a firm mango
caster sugar

4 oz (100 g) plain flour
1 egg, separated
¼ pint (150 ml) milk
deep oil for frying

Prepare the fruit; the manner depends on which type you are using. Peel, quarter and core the apples and cut into thick slices. Cut the bananas into 2 inch (5 cm) lengths. Halve apricots and remove the stone. Halve the mango, remove the stone, peel off the skin and cut into slices. Sprinkle with caster sugar.

Put the flour in a bowl, making a well in the centre. Blend the egg yolk with the milk and then add it to the flour to make a thick smooth batter.

Whisk the egg white until it is stiff and then fold it into the batter.

Heat the oil to 375°F, 190°C in a large pan, dip the fruit in the batter, one piece at a time, then fry until golden brown. Drain on kitchen paper and serve at once with sugar and cream, or try lemon juice if you do not have a sweet tooth.

# Toffee Apples

Makes 6

*Toffee apples are fairly easy to make and perfect for children's parties. Wrap them in cellophane and decorate with a pretty ribbon.*

6 small eating apples
6 wooden skewers or lolly sticks
8 oz (225 g) demerara sugar

1 oz (25 g) butter
1 teaspoon vinegar
4 tablespoons water
1 level tablespoon golden syrup

Wash the apples and dry them thoroughly on kitchen paper. Remove the stalks and push a wooden skewer or lolly stick firmly into each apple.

Put the sugar, butter, vinegar, water and syrup into a heavy-based pan and heat gently until the sugar has dissolved. Then boil rapidly for about 5 minutes until the temperature reaches 290 °F, 143 °C on a sugar thermometer, or until a little mixture, when placed in cold water, forms a very hard ball and is brittle.

Remove from the heat immediately and quickly dip in the apples to coat, then dip them in cold water to set the outside. Place on a sheet of waxed paper and leave to set.

When firm, wrap in cellophane or cling film and decorate with a ribbon.

## Green Fruit Salad

Serves 8

*I now rarely make a fruit syrup (see page 192). I find that if you layer the fruit with caster sugar the day before, the fruits make their own syrup; you can flavour it with liqueur or lemon juice if you like. If you put lemon juice on the apples they will retain their colour, but always add bananas just before serving the salad.*

2 Granny Smith apples, cored
   and sliced
2 pears, peeled, cored and sliced
juice of 1 lemon
8 oz (225 g) caster sugar
8 oz (225 g) large green grapes,
   seeded

2 kiwi fruits, peeled and sliced
1 small melon, peeled, seeded
   and cut into cubes
4 fresh figs, peeled and sliced
4 lychees, peeled and stoned

Place the apples and pears in a bowl and squeeze over the juice of the lemon to prevent discolouration. Sprinkle with some of the sugar and then cover with another layer of fruit and some more sugar. Continue until all the fruit has been added, finishing with a layer of sugar.

Cover the bowl and leave overnight in the refrigerator.

Turn into a glass serving dish, mixing lightly so that all the fruits are blended evenly. Serve with plenty of cream.

# Parisienne Flan

*This is a classic French open tart and is at its best served warm on the day that it is made.*

6 oz (175 g) plain flour
2 oz (50 g) butter
1½ oz (40 g) lard
1 large egg yolk
1 oz (25 g) caster sugar
about 2 teaspoons cold water

**Filling:**
1½ lb (675 g) cooking apples
3 tablespoons cold water
about 3 tablespoons granulated
    sugar
apricot jam
2 red-skinned eating apples for
    topping

First make the pastry: put the flour in a bowl, add the fats, cut into small pieces, and rub them in with the fingertips until the mixture resembles fine breadcrumbs. Mix the egg yolk with the sugar and water and stir into the dry ingredients to bind.

Roll out the pastry on a floured surface and line a 9 inch (22.5 cm) flan ring, which is standing on a baking sheet. Chill in the refrigerator for 30 minutes.

Heat the oven to 425 °F, 220 °C, gas mark 6. Line the flan with greaseproof paper, weigh down with baking beans and bake blind for 15 minutes.

Meanwhile prepare the filling: wash the apples and then quarter, core and slice them into a saucepan, together with the water. Cover and cook gently until the apples are soft and fluffy, about 15 minutes, stirring occasionally to prevent them catching.

Sieve the apples into a bowl and stir in the sugar and sweeten to taste.

Remove the beans and greaseproof paper from the flan and spoon in the apple filling.

Warm a little apricot jam in a saucepan so that it will form a glaze. If necessary add a little water and sieve it to make it smooth.

Cut the eating apples into quarters, core and thinly slice them. Arrange the slices in an attractive pattern on top of the apple purée. Brush all over with the apricot glaze.

Return the flan to the oven. Reduce the temperature to 350 °F, 180 °C, gas mark 4 and bake for a further 20 to 25 minutes, until the pastry is pale brown and the slices of apple are cooked.

Serve warm with cream.

# Apple and Hazelnut Flan

Serves 4

*The hazelnut pastry makes this apple flan rather special.*

*Pastry:*
4 oz (100 g) plain flour
2 oz (50 g) butter
1 oz (25 g) caster sugar
1 oz (25 g) hazelnuts, chopped
1 egg yolk
2 teaspoons cold water

*Filling:*
12 oz (350 g) cooking apples
1 oz (25 g) granulated sugar
1 to 2 red-skinned eating apples,
  cored and thinly sliced
2 tablespoons apricot jam
1 tablespoon water

Heat the oven to 425 °F, 220 °C, gas mark 7.

Measure the flour into a bowl and rub in the butter until the mixture resembles breadcrumbs. Stir in the sugar and hazelnuts. Blend the egg yolk with the water and stir into the dry ingredients and bind together.

Roll out the pastry on a floured surface and line a 7 inch (17.5 cm) fluted flan ring or a baking sheet. Bake blind in the oven for 15 minutes (see Parisienne Flan, page 28).

Meanwhile, peel, core and chop the cooking apples and place them in a saucepan over a low heat together with the sugar. Cook gently, stirring until the apples are soft and fluffy. Beat the apples until smooth.

Remove the paper and beans from the flan and return it to the oven for a further 5 minutes to dry out the pastry base. Then spoon the apple mixture into the flan. Arrange the sliced apple attractively on top of the purée.

Heat the jam and water together to form a syrup and spoon this over the flan.

Reduce the heat to 400 °F, 200 °C, gas mark 6 and return the flan to the oven for a further 10 to 15 minutes.

Leave the flan to cool on the baking sheet, then transfer it to a serving dish. If liked, decorate it with a little whipped cream and a few whole hazelnuts.

# Cider Apple Sauce

Serves 4

*A simple sauce to make and very good with pork, mackerel or herrings.*

12 oz (350 g) cooking apples
1 oz (25 g) butter
3 tablespoons cider vinegar

¼ pint (150 ml) cider
1 level tablespoon sugar

Peel, core and chop the apples and put in a saucepan together with all the remaining ingredients.

Cover and then simmer gently for about 20 minutes, or until the apples are soft. Stir occasionally during cooking time, then remove from the heat and beat well until the mixture is thick and pulpy.

Serve with roast pork or grilled chops or sausages. This sauce is also good served with grilled mackerel or herrings.

# Apple and Mint Jelly

Makes about 3 lb (1.4 kg)

*This is a really good, fresh tasting jelly which makes an excellent accompaniment to roast lamb.*

3 lb (1.4 kg) cooking apples
1 lemon
1½ pints (900 ml) boiling water

granulated sugar
1 bunch mint
green colouring

Wash the fruit. Slice the apples and lemon, including the peel, core and pips. Place them in a saucepan with the water, then cover and simmer slowly for 30 minutes or until the apples are very soft and pulpy. Mash well with a potato masher. Tip into a jelly bag and strain for at least 2 hours or overnight.

Measure the strained juice, and for each pint (600 ml) allow 1 lb (450 g) granulated sugar.

Place the sugar and juice in a saucepan. Reserve the small tender mint leaves and chop very finely. Tie the remainder in a bunch and lower them into the juice and sugar. Bring to the boil and boil quickly until setting point is reached. (See Crab Apple Jelly page 61.)

Lift out the bunch of mint and discard. Colour the jelly lightly with a few drops of green colouring and stir in the chopped mint. Continue to stir the jelly until it starts to thicken slightly and the mint no longer floats on the surface or sinks to the bottom of the saucepan.

Pot quickly into small jars, cover with waxed paper and, when cold, cover with screw-top lids or cellophane covers.

## Apple Relish
Makes about 3lb (1.4 kg)

*This relish improves if kept for about 1 month before opening.*

2 lb (900 g) cooking apples, peeled and cored (weighed after preparation)
1 large onion
3 tablespoons wine vinegar
12 oz (350 g) dark soft brown sugar
1 rounded teaspoon mustard seed

grated rind and juice of 1 lemon
3 bay leaves
4 oz (100 g) raisins, roughly chopped
1 level tablespoon salt
$\frac{1}{4}$ level teaspoon chilli powder
2 level teaspoons ground ginger
4 cloves garlic, crushed

Mince the apples and onion and place in a thick-bottomed saucepan together with the vinegar, sugar, mustard seed, lemon rind and bay leaves. Simmer gently, stirring occasionally, for about 20 minutes until the fruit is soft.

Add the remaining ingredients and stir well together. Bring to the boil and then reduce the heat and simmer, stirring occasionally, until the mixture is of a fairly thick, chutney-like consistency. This will take about 45 to 60 minutes.

Discard the bay leaves and pot in clean warm jars. Seal with plastic or vinegar-proof lids.

# Apple and Green Tomato Chutney

Makes about 10 lb (4.5 kg)

*An excellent way of using up windfall apples, and also green tomatoes. The red pepper gives an interesting splash of colour.*

2 lb (900 g) onions, chopped
5 lb (2.3 kg) green tomatoes, sliced
2 red peppers, seeded and chopped
2 lb (900 g) cooking apples, peeled, cored and sliced
8 oz (225 g) chopped raisins
2 inch (5 cm) piece fresh root ginger, peeled and finely chopped

1½ oz (40 g) salt
½ level teaspoon chilli powder
1 level teaspoon ground cummin
2 lb (900 g) muscovado brown sugar
6 cloves garlic, crushed
1½ pints (900 ml) malt vinegar

Put all the ingredients in a large saucepan and bring to the boil, stirring continually. Simmer, uncovered, for 2 to 3 hours, stirring occasionally. When ready, the fruit and vegetables should be soft and the mixture of a pulpy, chutney-like, consistency.

Pour into warm jars and cover with plastic or vinegar-proof lids.

# Apple, Tomato and Ginger Chutney

Makes about 4½ lb (2 kg)

*This is a good basic chutney that goes well with anything. Green ginger, which is much used in Chinese cooking, is available from better greengrocers. It looks knobbly.*

3 lb (1.4 kg) ripe tomatoes
1 lb (450 g) cooking apples, peeled, cored and chopped
12 oz (350 g) onions, peeled and chopped
3 oz (75 g) green ginger

1 oz (25 g) garlic, peeled
1 level tablespoon salt
1 pint distilled malt vinegar
1 lb (450 g) soft brown sugar
½ level teaspoon cayenne pepper
1 level teaspoon ground cloves

Plunge the tomatoes into boiling water for 10 seconds, then drain them and peel off the skins. Put the skinned tomatoes into a large pan together with the apples and onions.

Put the green ginger into a bowl, pour boiling water over it and leave for 5 minutes. Drain off the water, peel the skin from the ginger and chop finely. Chop the garlic roughly, then crush it on a wooden board with salt until no large lumps remain. Add the ginger, garlic, salt and vinegar to the pan. Cover and simmer for 30 minutes, or until the ingredients are tender. Remove the lid and continue to cook the chutney for a further 15 minutes, stirring frequently, until some of the liquid has evaporated and the mixture is a thin pulp.

Add the sugar, cayenne pepper and cloves and let the chutney continue to simmer, stirring frequently, for about 25 minutes, until it reaches a thick chutney-like consistency.

Pour into clean hot jars and cover with plastic or vinegar-proof lids and seal.

# Apricot

In a hilltop village in the English Midlands each of the ancient cottages has an apricot tree growing up its stone walls, against which the golden fruit ripen among the dark leaves in the late summer warmth. It is said that the villagers once used the apricots to pay the tolls due to the Lord of the Manor.

Most of the apricots we eat today come, from May to July, from the warm Mediterranean countries, or, between September and February, from Australia and South Africa.

The apricot is a small, stone fruit with orange-yellow, juicy, sweet flesh. It should be eaten when slightly soft to the touch. Avoid any with bruised skins. Those with a greenish tinge are unlikely to ripen after purchase.

Eat apricots as a dessert fruit or use them in puddings and pies and in preserves. Make them into apricot fool or add them to fruit salad. Do not throw away the stones; the kernels add an attractive flavour to jams and chutneys.

When freezing apricots it is wise to remove the skins because these can toughen during the process. Plunge the fruit into boiling water for 30 seconds, then put them into cold water; the skins will come off easily. You can cook and freeze the fruit either whole or as a purée for use in flans and puddings. Allow apricots to thaw before cooking and they will keep their colour. You can also buy them canned or dried.

# Chilled Apricot Soufflé

Serves 6

*The mixture for a cold soufflé and for a mousse is exactly the same; it just depends on what kind of dish you want to serve it from. If you like, pour this mixture into a glass dish and call it a mousse!*

1 lb (450 g) fresh apricots
4 tablespoons cold water
thinly peeled rind and juice of half a lemon
5 oz (150 g) caster sugar
½ oz (12.5 g) powdered gelatine

3 large eggs, separated
1 tablespoon apricot brandy or brandy
¼ pint (150 ml) double cream
¼ pint (150 ml) single cream

Measure a piece of greaseproof paper or non-stick paper three times as deep as a 1½ pint (900 ml) soufflé dish and large enough to go round the outside of it. Fold the paper in half lengthwise, then fold over a ½ inch (1.25 cm) strip along the folded edge. Put the paper around the outside of the dish so that the folded part is at the base. Secure the top of the paper collar with a paper clip and then tie a piece of string very firmly around the paper and dish.

Wash the apricots, then place them in a pan with 1 tablespoon of water, lemon peel and 2 oz (50 g) of sugar. Cover the pan with a well-fitting lid and simmer the apricots until they are tender. Remove the lemon peel, cut the apricots in half, remove the stones and sieve. This will yield about ½ pint (300 ml) apricot purée.

Put the gelatine and remaining 3 tablespoons of water into a small bowl or cup and stand it in hot water until it is dissolved and clear.

Put the egg yolks, remaining sugar and lemon juice into a fairly large bowl. Place this over a pan of hot water and whisk with a rotary whisk until the mixture is thick and pale in colour.

Remove from the heat and whisk in the apricot purée and dissolved gelatine, together with the apricot brandy. Leave in a cool place, stirring occasionally until thick but not set.

Meanwhile whisk the two creams together until the mixture will just form soft peaks. Fold into the thickened apricot mixture. Whisk the egg whites until they are stiff and then fold them into the mixture. Pour into the soufflé dish and leave in a refrigerator to set, preferably overnight.

When required, remove the paper very carefully by working away from the sides of soufflé with the back of a knife.

# Beef with Apricots

Serves 4

*As a variation, make this dish with stewing lamb.*

1½ lb (675 g) stewing steak
1 oz (25 g) dripping
2 onions, chopped
2 level teaspoons paprika
  pepper
1 oz (25 g) flour
½ pint (300 ml) stock

1 level teaspoon salt
ground black pepper
1 level teaspoon demerara
  sugar
1 tablespoon malt vinegar
8 oz (225 g) fresh apricots
4 oz (100 g) frozen peas

Cut the meat into neat 1 inch (2.5 cm) cubes. Melt the dripping in a pan and add the meat and onions and fry quickly for 2 minutes. Stir in the paprika pepper and flour and cook for 1 minute.

Add the stock, seasoning, sugar and vinegar and bring to the boil, stirring. Then reduce the heat, cover the saucepan and simmer gently for about 1½ hours.

Stone and halve or quarter the apricots. Add these to the pan and cook for 30 minutes. Add peas 15 minutes before the end of cooking time. Taste and check seasoning. Turn into a serving dish and serve very hot with plain boiled noodles.

# Apricot Curried Sausages

Serves 4

*Sausages are very much a British stand-by and this is a good variation on a familiar theme.*

½ oz (12.5 g) dripping
1 lb (450 g) pork sausages
1 onion, chopped
1 level tablespoon mild curry
  powder
2 level tablespoons flour
¾ pint (450 ml) stock

8 oz (225 g) apricots, halved
  and stoned
1 cooking apple, peeled, cored
  and diced
1 green pepper, seeded and
  sliced
1 tablespoon lemon juice
salt and pepper

Melt the dripping in a frying pan, add the sausages and fry quickly to brown on all sides. Lift them out and keep warm.

Add the onion to the fat in the pan and fry for 2 to 3 minutes. Stir in the curry powder and flour and cook for 2 minutes. Add the stock and bring to the boil, stirring until the sauce has thickened.

Return the sausages to the pan, together with the remaining ingredients and then simmer gently uncovered, for 30 minutes.

Taste, check seasoning and serve with plain boiled rice.

# Apricot Mousse
Serves 8

*This is a first-rate mousse made with dried apricots and it is deliciously sharp. You can use apricot pieces, which are cheaper than whole apricots. Dried peaches could be used instead of apricots.*

| | |
|---|---|
| 8 oz (225 g) dried apricots | 4 oz (100 g) caster sugar |
| 1 pint (600 ml) boiling water | juice of 1 lemon |
| 4 tablespoons cold water | 3 egg whites |
| ½ oz (100 g) powdered gelatine | ¼ pint (150 ml) double cream |

Wash the apricots, put in a saucepan and pour boiling water over them. Cover the saucepan with a lid and leave to soak for 2 hours.

Place the pan over a low heat, bring to the boil and then simmer gently for 30 minutes or until the apricots are tender. Keep the pan covered during cooking time and add a little extra water if too much should boil away, although this is not usually necessary. The apricots need to be just covered.

Meanwhile put the cold water in a cup or basin, sprinkle in the gelatine and leave to soak. When the apricots are soft, draw the pan from the heat and stir in the gelatine and sugar until they are completely dissolved.

Sieve the apricots to make a purée and discard the skins. Add the lemon juice and leave the mixture on one side until it is cool and beginning to thicken.

Whisk the egg whites until they are stiff. Whisk the cream until it forms soft peaks, then fold into the apricot purée and, lastly, carefully fold in the egg whites.

Turn into a glass serving dish and chill until firm before serving.

# Fresh Apricot Tart

Serves 8

*This tart has a very light filling – it is really a rich apricot cream custard. It is best served on the day that it is made. You could use plums or damsons instead of apricots.*

6 oz (175 g) flour
1½ oz (40 g) margarine
1½ oz (40 g) lard
about 6 teaspoons cold water to
   mix

**Filling:**
8 oz (225 g) stoned apricots
2 level tablespoons caster sugar
2 large eggs, separated
¼ pint (150 ml) double cream

Put the flour in a bowl, add the margarine and lard cut into small pieces and rub these into the flour with the fingertips until the mixture resembles fine breadcrumbs. Add just sufficient cold water to mix to a firm dough. Roll out the pastry fairly thinly and use to line a 9 inch (22.5 cm) metal flan dish. Chill in the refrigerator for 15 minutes.

Meanwhile place the apricots in a single layer in a saucepan, sprinkle with the sugar but do not add water. Cook very gently over a low heat until they are soft and then sieve into a bowl and leave to cool.

Heat the oven to 425 °F, 220 °C, gas mark 7 and place a baking sheet in it. Line the flan with a piece of greaseproof paper, weigh it down with baking beans and then bake blind on the baking sheet for 15 minutes. Remove the paper and beans from the flan and reduce the oven temperature to 350 °F, 180 °C, gas mark 4.

Beat the egg yolks into the apricot purée with the cream. Whisk the egg whites until they are stiff and fold them into the apricot mixture. Spoon into the flan and bake in the oven for 25 to 35 minutes until the filling is set.

# Avocado

The avocado's only connection with the pear is its shape. There are several varieties of avocado, some with a rough, shiny, bright-green skin, others rough and wrinkled and almost black when ready for eating. Avocados come from Israel, South Africa and America and are available all the year round. The flesh is pale green and creamy in texture with a delicate flavour which lends itself to the addition of piquant sauces. The large smooth stone in the centre of the fruit leaves a convenient cavity to hold accompaniments.

Avocados are usually eaten as a first course. Serve them with prawns in mayonnaise, or fill the cavity with vinaigrette. Or, even more simply, serve with Worcestershire sauce (real devotees swear by this). Use avocados in a salad or make them into a delicious soup.

The fruit is harvested and exported before it is ripe. However, eat avocados only when they are ripe, otherwise they are hard and tasteless. To test for ripeness, place the fruit in the palm of your hand and squeeze gently. It should give a little all over. To ripen avocados quickly, put them in a warm place in the kitchen or in an airing cupboard. Once ripe they will keep in the salad drawer of the refrigerator for up to four days.

Be careful when preparing them. Using a stainless steel knife, make a level cut lengthwise, encircling the fruit and reaching to the stone. Separate the halves by rotating them in opposite directions. Extract the stone by lifting the pointed end with the tip of a knife. Sprinkle the flesh with lemon juice to prevent it discolouring. Incidentally, the skin, if rubbed over the hands, is a good beauty treatment.

Freeze as a purée, with lemon juice added.

Recipes:
Baked Avocados with Crab, 40
Avocado Pears with Prawns, 40
Avocado Vinaigrette, 41
Chicken and Avocado Salad, 41
Avocado and Pork Salad, 42
Avocado Mousse, 42
Guacamole, 43
Avocado and Strawberry Mille Feuille, 44

# Baked Avocados with Crab

Serves 3 or 6

*This makes a delicious first course or light lunch. Use frozen crab meat. It is more reasonable in price than canned crab and has a better flavour.*

1 oz (25 g) butter
1 oz (25 g) flour
¼ pint (150 ml) milk
4 to 6 oz (100 to 175 g) flaked
   crab meat

1 level tablespoon tomato
   purée
salt and pepper
3 ripe avocado pears
lemon juice

Heat the oven to 350 °F, 180 °C, gas mark 4.

Melt the butter in a small saucepan, stir in the flour and cook for 1 minute, then blend in the milk and bring to the boil, stirring. Simmer for 2 minutes and then stir in the crab meat, tomato purée and seasoning to taste.

Cut the avocado pears in half lengthwise and remove the stones. Score the flesh with a knife and sprinkle with lemon juice and a little salt to preserve the colour. Pile the crab mixture on top of the pears, spreading it so that all the pear is covered. Stand the pears in an ovenproof dish and add about 1 inch (2.5 cm) boiling water and bake in the oven for 30 minutes.

Serve with chunks of French bread or warm granary rolls. One half pear makes an excellent first course; for a light lunch, serve two per person.

# Avocado Pears with Prawns

Serves 6

*If you like a slightly more piquant filling, add 1 tablespoon of horse-radish cream to the mixture. It goes very well.*

3 ripe avocado pears
2 rounded tablespoons
   mayonnaise
2 tablespoons double cream
1 tablespoon tomato ketchup

Worcestershire sauce
juice of half a lemon
6 to 8 oz (175 to 225 g) peeled
   prawns
paprika pepper

Chill the avocados in the bottom of the refrigerator for about 1 hour before you plan to serve them.

Place the mayonnaise, cream, ketchup, a drop or two of Worcestershire sauce and the lemon juice in a bowl and mix well together. Stir in the prawns and chill in the refrigerator.

When required, cut the avocados in half lengthwise and remove the stones. Rub the flesh with a little lemon juice to prevent discolouration; I use the squeezed half lemon for this. Place the pears on a serving dish.

Taste the prawn mixture and, if necessary, adjust the seasoning. Then spoon the mixture into the centre of the pears. Sprinkle each with a little paprika pepper.

## Avocado Vinaigrette

Prepare the pears as above and serve with a little vinaigrette dressing spooned into the centre of each.

## Chicken and Avocado Salad                    Serves 4

*This is a delicious summer salad.*

12 oz (350 g) cooked chicken,
  diced
1 large avocado pear
¼ pint (150 ml) mayonnaise
salt
freshly ground black pepper

1 teaspoon lemon juice, or to
  taste
lettuce
cucumber and tomato slices, to
  garnish

Cut the avocado pear in half and remove the stone. Scoop out the flesh and chop roughly.

Mash half the avocado flesh and mix with the mayonnaise, salt, pepper and lemon juice. Stir in the remaining avocado and the diced chicken. Taste and check the seasoning.

Arrange a bed of lettuce on a serving dish, pile the avocado and chicken mayonnaise in the centre and garnish with sliced cucumber and tomato.

# Avocado and Pork Salad

Serves 4

*Avocado pears go very well in salads. The addition of sliced beetroot makes this a very colourful and nutritious lunch.*

2 ripe avocado pears
lemon juice
2 tablespoons apple juice
2 tablespoons horseradish
  sauce

2 tablespoons mayonnaise
salt
freshly ground black pepper
6 small beetroot, sliced
8 slices cold pork
small sprigs of watercress

Peel the avocado pears, cut them in half and remove the stones and then brush all over with lemon juice to prevent discolouration.

Blend the apple juice, horseradish sauce and mayonnaise together and season to taste. Spoon the mixture into the avocado halves.

Line the edge of a flat dish with the sliced beetroot and arrange the pork down the centre of the dish. Put the avocado pears on top and garnish with small sprigs of watercress.

# Avocado Mousse

Serves 4 to 6

*For very special occasions serve decorated with peeled prawns and chervil and accompanied by thinly sliced bread and butter.*

½ oz (12.5 g) gelatine
4 tablespoons cold water
¼ pint (150 ml) boiling water
1 chicken stock cube
2 large ripe avocado pears
1 level teaspoon salt
½ level teaspoon ground black
  pepper

1 tablespoon lemon juice
piece of onion the size of a
  walnut, crushed in a garlic
  press
½ pint (300 ml) mayonnaise
¼ pint (150 ml) double cream,
  lightly whipped

Place the gelatine and cold water in a small bowl or cup. Let it stand for 3 minutes until the mixture becomes sponge-like, then place the bowl in a pan of simmering water and allow the gelatine to dissolve. Stir the boiling water and stock cube together until the cube has dissolved and then stir in the gelatine.

Peel and quarter the avocados, remove the stones and then crush the flesh with a fork and push it through a nylon sieve. Stir in the stock, together with salt, pepper, lemon juice and the onion. Leave to become quite cold and then fold in the mayonnaise and cream.

Pour into a 2 pint (a good litre-sized) serving dish and leave in the refrigerator to set.

If liked, decorate with cucumber slices and a little piped mayonnaise.

## Guacamole

*This is a speciality dish from Mexico and makes two avocados go a long way.*

1 level teaspoon salt
¼ level teaspoon freshly ground black pepper
1 level teaspoon made mustard
2 level teaspoons caster sugar
6 tablespoons salad oil
2 tablespoons lemon juice
2 ripe avocado pears
2 tomatoes, skinned, seeded and chopped
4 spring onions, chopped

Put the salt, pepper, mustard and sugar into a small bowl. Blend in the oil a little at a time, then blend in the lemon juice.

Cut the avocado pears in half, remove the stone and scoop out the flesh into another bowl. Mash it with a fork until it is smooth. If it has to be kept waiting put the stones with it to prevent it discolouring and turning black.

Blend in the dressing slowly and then, finally, fold in the tomato and spring onion.

Turn the guacamole into a tureen or bowl and serve with Chilli con Carne or, on its own, as a first course or as a dip.

# Avocado and Strawberry Mille Feuille

Serves 6 to 8

*This dessert cake tastes as good as it looks. It is surprisingly easy to make.*

14 oz (397 g) packet puff
   pastry, thawed
4 tablespoons strawberry jam
8 oz (225 g) strawberries,
   hulled and cut in halves
   lengthways

*Icing:*
4 oz (100 g) icing sugar, sieved
about 1 tablespoon warm water
a few drops of green colouring

*Sweet avocado cream:*
2 ripe avocado pears
a little icing sugar
4 tablespoons stiffly whisked
   double cream
2 teaspoons lime juice or rum
   or brandy

Heat the oven to 425 °F, 220 °C, gas mark 7.

Roll out the pastry to an oblong 11 by 12 inches (27.5 by 30 cm) and trim the edges. Cut into two oblongs, each 5½ by 12 inches (14 by 30 cm). Lift on to a baking sheet and make a criss-cross pattern on top of one piece of pastry using a sharp knife.

Bake the pastry in the oven for 15 minutes until it is well risen and golden brown. Lift off the baking sheet and leave to cool on a wire rack. Split each piece in half.

Cut the avocado pears in half and remove the stones. Scoop out the flesh into a bowl and mash it with a fork until it is smooth. Stir in the icing sugar to taste and then add the cream and a little lime juice, rum or brandy.

Place one piece of pastry on a serving plate and spread it with half the sweet avocado cream. Cover with another piece of pastry and spread with jam and cover with a layer of strawberries, cut side down. Put a third piece of pastry on top and spread with the remaining cream. Finally cover with a scored piece of pastry.

Blend the icing sugar with warm water and a little green colouring to make a thin glacé icing. Pour over the top and allow any surplus to trickle down the sides.

# Banana

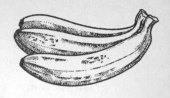

Two kinds of banana are eaten in this country – the *Jamaica*, which is long and fairly large with a mild flavour, and the *Canary*, which is smaller with a more pronounced flavour. Bananas are imported in large bunches while still green and are ripened in special warehouses before appearing in the shops. They are available all the year round.

When the skin turns a golden yellow the fruit is just ripe, but it is as its best when brown spots appear on the skin. This period of perfection does not last long, so it is wise to buy bananas in small quantities as you need them. You can buy them unripe and ripen them at room temperature, being careful to keep them away from draughts. The banana is a delicate fruit that bruises easily and is to be treated with care.

Eat bananas as a dessert fruit or use them in cooked sweets, such as Fruit Fritters, or flambéed with rum. They can also be used to accompany savoury dishes – Chicken Maryland, for example.

Do not freeze the banana whole, or even put it in the refrigerator. The texture does not survive thawing. Purée it in the blender with sugar, freeze it and use for cake and sandwich fillings.

# Banana Rolls

Serves 4

*There is no need to make batter for this recipe. Just use fairly thinly rolled out puff pastry; it gives a lovely crisp coating to the bananas.*

8 oz (227 g) packet puff pastry,
  thawed
4 firm bananas

juice of 1 lemon
deep fat or oil for frying
caster sugar

Roll out the pastry to an oblong 12 by 9 inches (30 cm by 22.5 cm), trim the edges and then cut the pastry into 8 strips, 1 inch (2.5 cm) wide and about 11 inches (27.5 cm) long. Damp each strip with water.

Peel the bananas and cut each across in half. Dip each piece of banana in lemon juice to prevent discolouration.

Wind a strip of pastry around each piece of banana so that it is completely enclosed and seal the ends firmly.

Heat the fat to hot – 340 °F (170 °C) – if you have a thermometer. If not, test with a cube of day-old bread which, at the required temperature, will sink to the bottom of the fat and then rise to the surface and brown in about 1 minute.

Fry the banana rolls in the fat for about 4 minutes until the pastry is golden brown and has puffed up. Lift out and drain on kitchen paper and then quickly toss in caster sugar. If liked serve with hot lemon sauce (see page 102).

# Hot Banana Pudding

Serves 6

*This recipe is one of the best ways I know of using up ripe bananas. It makes a simply delicious pudding.*

6 ripe bananas
2 oz (50 g) butter
4 oz (100 g) caster sugar

4 oz (100 g) self-raising flour
1 egg, beaten
generous pinch mixed spice

Heat the oven to 350 °F, 180 °C, gas mark 4. Butter a 1¾ pint (1 litre) ovenproof dish.

Place the bananas in a large bowl and mash to a pulp. Melt the butter and stir into the bananas. Add the sugar, flour, egg and mixed spice and mix together thoroughly. Turn into the prepared dish and bake in the oven for 40 to 50 minutes, until the pudding is golden brown and has shrunk slightly from the sides of the dish.

Serve hot with cream.

# Just Fried Bananas

Serves 4

*One of the simplest hot puddings to make and very popular with children.*

2 oz (50 g) butter          2 oz (50 g) demerara sugar
4 small bananas

Melt the butter in a large frying pan.

Peel the bananas and cut each into two across the middle. Put them in the frying pan and fry for 2 to 3 minutes until they are a light golden brown, turning constantly.

Lift out onto a warm serving dish and sprinkle with demerara sugar.

Serve at once with a dollop of thick cream.

# Honey and Banana Creams

Serves 4 to 6

*A simple and effective pudding. To make it slightly more special, add 2 tablespoons brandy to the banana mixture.*

4 ripe bananas                       juice of half a lemon
2 to 3 level tablespoons thin        ½ pint (300 ml) whipping cream
  honey                              walnut halves

Mash the bananas with honey and lemon juice until the mixture is fairly smooth.

Whisk the cream until it forms soft peaks and then, with a spoon, gently fold in the mashed banana mixture.

Turn into a 2 pint (1 litre) glass serving dish. Chill for 2 hours and then serve, decorated with a few walnut halves.

# Banana Flapjacks

Makes 16 flapjacks

*A very good way of using up slightly over-ripe bananas.*

3 oz (75 g) butter
2 tablespoons golden syrup
4 oz (100 g) demerara sugar

1 large banana, mashed
6 oz (175 g) rolled outs

Heat the oven to 350 °F, 180 °C, gas mark 4. Grease a 7 by 11 inch (17.5 by 27.5 cm) Swiss roll tin.

Put the butter, golden syrup and demerara sugar in a saucepan and heat gently until the butter has melted and the sugar dissolved. Remove the pan from the heat and stir in the banana and oats and mix thoroughly.

Press into the tin and then bake in the oven for about 35 to 40 minutes until the flapjack mixture is a pale golden brown. Remove from the oven and leave to cool for 15 minutes in the tin and then mark into 16 fingers and allow to finish cooling in the tin. Lift out and store in airtight tin.

# Chocolate Banana Tarts

Serves 8

*If time is short, use bought pastry cases and then fill them with the cream and bananas, and then top with chocolate. Bananas and chocolate make a marvellous combination.*

4 oz (100 g) plain flour
2½ oz (62 g) butter
½ oz (12.5 g) caster sugar
about 4 teaspoons cold water

Filling:
¼ pint (150 ml) whipping cream
2 bananas
3 oz (75 g) chocolate

Heat the oven to 375 °F, 190 °C, gas mark 5.

Put the flour in a bowl, add the butter, cut into small pieces, and rub in until the mixture resembles fine breadcrumbs. Stir in the sugar and sufficient cold water to mix to a firm dough. Roll out the pastry on a lightly floured surface and cut out, with a 3 inch (7.5 cm) fluted cutter, 16 circles and use these to line tart tins. Prick very well and then chill in the refrigerator for 10 minutes. Bake in the oven for 10 to 15 minutes and then remove and leave to cool on a wire rack.

Whisk the cream until it is thick and then divide it between the tarts. Slice the bananas and place three slices on each tart on top of the cream.

Break the chocolate into pieces, place these in a bowl and stand it over a pan of simmering water until the chocolate is melted and smooth.

Make a small bag of greaseproof paper and cut a small piece off the tip. Fill with the chocolate and then pipe a trail of chocolate backwards and forwards over each tart. Leave to set; this will take about 1 hour.

## Banana and Mandarin Yogurt
Serves 2

1 ripe banana          2 mandarins
¼ pint (150 ml) natural yogurt

Peel and mash the banana in a bowl and stir in the yogurt.

Peel the mandarins, remove any fine white pith and put 6 segments on one side for decoration. Cut the remainder in half and remove any pips. Add to the yogurt and mix well. Divide the mixture between two glasses or dishes and arrange the whole segments on top.

Chill the yogurt in the refrigerator for about an hour before serving.

## Banana and Apple Yogurt
Serves 2

Make as above but use a crisp eating apple instead of the mandarins. Peel, core and finely dice the apple and add it to the mixture. Sprinkle with dark soft brown sugar and serve.

## Banana Cake Filling

Chopped banana and whipped cream make an excellent cake filling. Chop or mash the banana and sprinkle it with a little lemon juice to prevent it discolouring. Then mix the banana with whipped cream and use to sandwich sponge cakes.

# Baked Bananas

Serves 4

*This must be one of the simplest of puddings to make. If the oven is still hot from cooking the main course, pop in a few bananas and they will be ready in time for pudding.*

4 bananas
¼ pint (150 ml) single cream

about 2 tablespoons
demerara sugar

Bake the bananas in a moderate oven for 10 to 15 minutes. The skins will turn black and the flesh become soft. Peel off the skins and serve with cream and a little demerara sugar.

# Bilberry

This is also the blaeberry, blueberry, whinberry or whortleberry. It grows wild on the hills of England, Scotland and Wales – and the purple juice soon transfers itself to the hands of younger members of the family who are sent out to pick berries.

The native berries are small, dark-blue or purple, with a grapelike bloom and a distinct flavour. Those sold in shops are larger, cultivated berries imported from America and Poland and sometimes from Norway. Their season is July to November.

Too acid to be served as a dessert fruit, bilberries are at their best in pies or tarts, preferably with lots of cream, or stewed or made into a jelly.

They can be stored in the freezer in strong polythene bags.

Bilberry recipe, see:
Rosy Red Fruit Pie, 161

# Blackberry

You can buy cultivated blackberries in the shops in late summer. They are bigger and juicier than the wild ones – but the wild ones are much more fun. The joy of an autumn day in the country spent picking your own fruit from the hedgerow is worth all the scratches that come with it.

Eat the berries as soon as you can after you get them home; they do not keep well and are apt to turn mushy. Wash them gently under running water and dry them on kitchen paper. Use them, along with apple, in a tart or a flan. If you do not like the seeds, heat the berries with a little water and sieve them. Do not forget that they make an excellent jelly, dark-purple and full of flavour.

You can freeze them, of course. The open method is best. Put the fruit on a tray until frozen, then pack in containers and seal.

# Blackberry Shortcake                    Serves 6

*This shortcake is equally delicious with loganberries, or a mixture of loganberries and raspberries.*

| | |
|---|---|
| 6 oz (175 g) butter | 3 oz (75 g) cornflour |
| 3 oz (75 g) caster sugar | 8 oz (225 g) blackberries |
| 6 oz (175 g) self-raising flour | 1 oz (25 g) demerara sugar |

Heat the oven to 375 °F, 190 °C, gas mark 5 and grease a 7 inch (17.5 cm) square shallow tin.

Cream the butter and sugar together until they are light and fluffy. Sift the flour and cornflour into a bowl, add to the creamed butter, work in and then knead together. Turn the mixture on to a surface and knead lightly for 3 minutes or until the mixture is smooth.

Reserve one-third of the mixture and spread the rest evenly over the base of the tin; use the flat of your hand to do this.

Cover with the blackberries. Add the demerara sugar to the reserved mixture and knead lightly until mixed. Pat it out roughly to the size of the tin and spread it over the blackberries. Bake in the oven for 45 minutes until the blackberries are cooked and the topping lightly browned.

Serve, with cream or ice cream, while the shortbread is still warm.

# Blackberry Snow

Serves 4 to 6

*You can also use this method to make a very good Apple Snow or Rhubarb Snow.*

| | |
|---|---|
| 1 lb (450 g) blackberries | 2 tablespoons water |
| 3 level tablespoons honey | 2 egg whites |

Put the blackberries into a saucepan with the honey and water. Cover the pan and cook gently for 10 minutes or until the fruit is soft, stirring occasionally. Remove from the heat and sieve the fruit into a large bowl, leave it to become cold and then chill it in the refrigerator.

Just before serving, whisk the egg whites until they are stiff and then fold them into the blackberry purée.

Turn the Snow into a glass serving dish. Serve immediately.

# Bramble Jelly

Makes 7 to 10 lb (3 to 4.5 kg)

*Store preserves in a cool, dark and dry cupboard and they will keep from one season through to the next.*

| | |
|---|---|
| 3 lb (1.4 kg) blackberries | 4 to 6 lb (1.8 to 2.7 kg) |
| 3 lb (1.4 kg) cooking apples | granulated sugar |
| 2 pints (a good litre) water | |

Wash the blackberries and apples. Chop the apples roughly, discarding any bad parts but leaving the core and peel. Place the fruit in a large saucepan and almost cover with the water. Cover the saucepan with a lid and simmer slowly for about 40 minutes until the fruit is soft and pulpy.

Mash the fruit well with a potato masher to ensure that it is really soft. Strain through a jelly bag for at least 2 hours or leave overnight.

Measure the juice, and for each pint (600 ml) allow 1 lb (450 g) granulated sugar.

Bring the juice to the boil and then stir in the sugar until dissolved. Boil quickly, removing any scum which forms with a slotted spoon. Boil until setting point is reached, about 10 to 12 minutes.

Pot and cover.

# Cape Gooseberry

Cape gooseberries, or Chinese lanterns, an exotic and rather improbable looking fruit, come from the Cape of Good Hope in South Africa. The papery thin, orange-coloured husks or 'lanterns' that cover the fruit are extremely decorative and the plant is much sought after by flower arrangers.

The fruit is yellow-green and not unlike the ordinary gooseberry, with many seeds. Remove the skin and eat it raw or serve it cooked in sweets and compôtes. The case or calyx can be bent back to form petals round the central berry to make an unusual decoration for cakes and sweets.

It is available from February to the end of March and keeps well for several weeks if unripe when bought.

# Cherry

Cherries can be divided into sweet and acid types and into white, red and black. Some are imported but the best are home-grown and the sight of a cherry orchard covered with blossom is one of the joys of spring. The fruit grows in clusters on longish stalks, making it very easy to pick and eat. The sweet dessert varieties have juicy flesh, varying from the pinkish-yellow of the white type to the dark-red of the black.

Home-grown cherries are at their best in June and July. Imported, they are in the shops from April to August. Morellos, dark-red and acid, are suitable for jam-making and are in season in July and August.

Buy firm and dry fruit and avoid containers with a high proportion of leaves to berries.

Eat cherries raw as dessert or, if they are to be cooked, wash them and remove stalks and stones. Cherries can be used in tarts, flans, as a sauce with roast duck, in fruit salad and with ice cream.

Choose ripe, sweet fruit to freeze. Red ones freeze better than black, and white ones should be frozen in syrup. Stones need not be removed.

# Bottled Black Cherries with Orange

Makes about 12 lb (6 kg)

*Bottle cherries for the store cupboard when they are at their cheapest.*

10 to 12 lb (4.5 to 6 kg) black cherries
rind of 2 oranges

4 pints (2.5 litres) water
1½ lb (675 g) granulated sugar

Wash the cherries and discard any bad ones. Remove the stalks and stone them with a cherry stoner, reserving any juice that runs from the fruit. If a cherry stoner is not available, use the tip of a swivel potato peeler to lift out the stones. It is not essential to stone cherries before bottling but it is helpful when you come to use them.

Pack the cherries quite tightly into jars to within ¾ inch (2 cm) of the tops of the jars.

Remove the rind from the oranges with a potato peeler, making sure that no white pith is removed. Place the rind in a saucepan with the water and sugar and any juice from the cherries. Bring very slowly to the boil, stirring until the sugar has dissolved. When boiling, quickly fill warmed jars to within ½ inch (1.25 cm) of the top. Add extra boiling water if there should be insufficient syrup to cover the fruit.

Place the lids on the jars. Rest the screw tops in place but *do not screw them down* as the contents will expand.

Stand the jars in a large roasting tin containing 1 inch (2.5 cm) of hot water. Place on a low shelf in the oven and cook at 300 °F, 150 °C, gas mark 2, until bubbles rise through the syrup. This will take from 1¼ to 1¾ hours.

Carefully remove the jars from the oven, one at a time, and at once screw down each lid very tightly. Wipe the jars with a warm damp cloth to remove any syrup from the outside. Leave to cool and then store until needed.

# Black Cherry Cheesecake

Serves 8

*Always a great favourite. Morello cherries are best in this recipe.*
*Buy them when they are at their cheapest in the summer. Damsons,*
*raspberries and strawberries are also excellent on a cheesecake.*

6 digestive biscuits, crushed
1½ oz (40 g) butter, melted
3 eggs, separated
4 oz (100 g) caster sugar
1 lb (450 g) cream cheese at
  room temperature

½ level teaspoon vanilla essence
1 lb (450 g) black cherries
  preferably stoned
3 tablespoons water
4 oz (125 g) caster sugar
1 rounded teaspoon arrowroot

Heat the oven to 350 °F, 180 °C, gas mark 4. Lightly butter and flour a 7
inch (17.5 cm) round loose-bottomed cake tin.

Blend the biscuits with the melted butter and press firmly over
the base of the cake tin.

Whisk the egg yolks and sugar until they are light and creamy and
stir in the cream cheese and vanilla essence until the mixture is well
blended.

Whisk the egg whites until they are stiff. Fold them into the cheese
mixture and spoon into the prepared tin.

Bake in the oven for about 1½ hours, until well risen and pale
golden brown and shrinking slightly away from the sides of the tin.
Then turn off the heat and leave in the oven for a further 15 to 30
minutes.

Remove from the oven and leave to cool in the tin until quite cold:
this cheesecake will sink slightly in the centre on cooling. Remove
from the tin and place on a serving dish.

Simmer the cherries in the water, sweetened with castor sugar.
Drain them, and, if necessary, stone them. Reserve the juice and
blend ¼ pint (150 ml) of it, with the arrowroot, in a small saucepan
and then slowly bring to the boil, stirring until thickened. Add the
cherries and mix lightly; spoon over the cheesecake and leave to
cool completely.

Chill before serving.

# Cherry Pancakes

Makes 8 to 10 pancakes

*Sweet pancakes are always popular.*

8 to 10 pancakes (see Crêpes
  Suzette, page 121)

*Filling:*
1 lb (450 g) black or red
  cherries
3 oz (75 g) granulated sugar, or
  to taste
4 oz (100 g) butter
1 level teaspoon cornflour
2 tablespoons water
caster sugar

Make the pancakes and put them on one side.

Remove the stalks from the cherries and take out the stones. Put the cherries in a saucepan and cook them gently with the sugar and 2 oz (50 g) butter, stirring occasionally, for about 20 minutes or until the cherries are tender. To thicken the filling, blend the cornflour with the water and add to the cherry mixture and stir over the heat until thickened.

Spread out the pancakes on a flat surface. Spoon the cherry filling on to the pancakes and then roll them up.

Melt the remaining butter in a frying pan and fry the rolled up pancakes on all sides until they are brown. Transfer them to a warm serving dish and sprinkle with caster sugar.

# Black Cherry Soufflé Omelette

Serves 2

*Omelettes are very quick to make, though we often think of them as a savoury dish. You can use this recipe to make a lemon soufflé omelette. Instead of the cold water put 2 teaspoons of lemon juice and the grated rind of the lemon in the omelette and sieve icing sugar over it just before serving. This is very good served with raspberries and cream.*

2 large eggs
1 dessertspoon caster sugar
2 teaspoons cold water
½ oz (12.5 g) butter

1 rounded tablespoon black
 cherry sauce 2 (see page 60)
icing sugar

Separate the eggs and place the yolks in a basin with the sugar and water; beat until pale and creamy.

Whisk the egg whites until they are just stiff. Mix 1 tablespoonful into the egg yolks and carefully fold in the remainder.

Heat an omelette pan and then, over a moderate heat, melt the butter in it. Spread the mixture into the pan and cook, without moving it, for 3 to 4 minutes until it is a pale golden brown underneath.

Slip the pan under a medium grill for 2 to 3 minutes to set the top. Make a slight cut across the centre of the omelette; spread one half with warmed black cherry sauce, fold it in half and slide it on to a warm serving dish. Dredge with icing sugar and serve at once.

## Cherry Dessert

To make a very simple dessert or topping for ice cream, stone the cherries and pour over brandy, Kirsch or gin. Sprinkle with sugar and leave to marinate overnight.

## Black Cherry Sauce (1)

*This is a good sauce to accompany duck or a hot ham dish or, of course, ice cream.*

15 oz (435 g) can pitted black
 cherries
2 level tablespoons cornflour

½ pint (300 ml) water
3 tablespoons sherry
sugar

Drain the juice from the cherries. Place the cornflour in a small saucepan and stir in the cherry juice and water and bring to the boil, stirring until the mixture has thickened. Add the sherry and, if liked, a very little sugar to taste. Simmer for a minute and then stir in the cherries.

Serve hot or cold.

# Black Cherry Sauce (2)

*A quick cheat recipe that can be served very successfully with roast duck.*

4 tablespoons black cherry jam    juice of half a lemon

Heat about 4 heaped tablespoons of black cherry jam in a small saucepan until it is melted and then add the juice of half a small lemon, or to taste.

# Crab Apple

The common crab is the original wild apple. There are a variety of cultivated types, making decorative trees in many an English garden. The fruit is apple-shaped, but much smaller, with a shiny red or yellow skin and firm flesh which is usually very sour. The season is September to October.

The crab apple is best used for making jelly, which is clear and of a good colour and goes well with various meats.

Store in the same way as ordinary apples.

## Crab Apple Jelly

Makes about 8 to 9 lb (3.6 to 4.1 kg)

6 lb (2.7 kg) crab apples
4 pints (2.3 litres) water
1 heaped teaspoon cloves

4 tablespoons lemon juice
granulated sugar

Wash the crab apples and remove all the leaves, stalks and any bruised parts. Place them in a preserving pan with the water, cloves and lemon juice. Bring to the boil and simmer for about 20 minutes or until the apples are soft. Mash well with a potato masher and leave to stand for about 20 minutes.

Pour into 2 jelly bags and leave to strain overnight.

Measure the juice and to each pint of juice (600 ml) allow 1 lb (450 g) granulated sugar. Place both in the preserving pan and bring to the boil, very slowly, stirring until the sugar has dissolved. Then boil fairly quickly for about 10 minutes or until setting point is reached. A small amount dropped on to a cold saucer will skin when pushed with a finger.

Remove from the heat and pour into clean warm jars. Cover and seal.

# Cranberry

Cranberries are small red berries similar to bilberries, and come mostly from America. They have hard flesh and small seeds and a sharp, slightly bitter flavour. They are available from October to February and are sold in punnets or polythene bags. They should last at least three weeks in the refrigerator, and unopened bags of fruit can be frozen for up to a year.

Very sour when eaten raw, they are usually cooked with sugar. Cook them only until they are just tender, or they will be bitter.

Recipes:

## Traditional Cranberry Sauce

*Sieve or blend the sauce if you prefer the texture of a purée. Serve with roast turkey, goose or pheasant.*

6 oz (175 g) caster sugar  
¼ pint (150 ml) water

8 oz (225 g) fresh cranberries

Put the sugar, together with the water, in a small saucepan and stir over a low heat until the sugar has dissolved.

Meanwhile wash the cranberries, remove any stalks and then add to the sugar syrup and bring slowly to the boil. Simmer gently for about 10 minutes or until the berries are tender, stirring occasionally. Remove from the heat and then turn into a small dish and serve warm.

# Cranberry and Banana Bread

*If very fresh this is fine to serve as a cake, but it may be wise to butter the last slices.*

6 oz (175 g) plain flour
3 level teaspoons baking
  powder
½ level teaspoon salt
5 oz (150 g) caster sugar
1 oz (25 g) walnuts
2 ripe bananas
1 egg, beaten
4 oz (100 g) butter, melted
2 level tablespoons whole berry
  cranberry sauce
3 oz (75 g) fresh cranberries

*Topping:*
2 level tablespoons whole berry
  cranberry sauce
1 oz (25 g) cranberries
1 level tablespoon honey,
  melted

Heat the oven to 350 °F, 180 °C, gas mark 4. Grease and line with greased greaseproof paper a 2 lb (900 g) loaf tin.

Sift the flour, baking powder and salt into a bowl, and add the sugar. Put 4 walnut halves on one side, chop the remaining nuts and add to the ingredients in the bowl.

Mash the bananas in a small bowl until smooth, then stir in the egg and melted butter, together with the cranberry sauce and fresh cranberries. Make a well in the centre of the dry ingredients, stir in the banana mixture and mix very thoroughly. Turn the mixture into the prepared tin and bake in the oven for about 1¼ to 1½ hours, or until a warm skewer inserted in the centre comes out clean.

Leave the bread to cool in the tin. When quite cold, turn out and remove the paper. Combine all the topping ingredients and spread over the top of the bread and place a walnut half in each corner.

# Cranberry and Apple Dessert Cake

Makes 8 to 10 slices

*This is a good way to use up any cranberries you have left over after Christmas or from whenever you have a turkey.*

2½ oz (62 g) butter
1 large egg
4 oz (100 g) caster sugar
½ teaspoon almond essence
4 oz (100 g) self-raising flour

scant level teaspoon baking powder
12 oz (350 g) cooking apples, before peeling
3 oz (75 g) cranberries
icing sugar

Heat the oven to 350 °F, 180 °C, gas mark 4. Well grease an 8 inch (20 cm) loose-bottomed cake tin.

Melt the butter in a saucepan until it is just runny and then pour it into a large bowl. Add the egg, sugar and almond essence and beat well until blended. Fold in the flour and baking powder. Spread just under two-thirds of the mixture in the tin. Then, straight away, peel, core and slice the apples and arrange roughly on top of the mixture. Sprinkle the cranberries over the top.

Spoon the remaining mixture over the apples. It is difficult to get this last bit of mixture smooth, but any blobs will even out during cooking.

Bake for 1¼ hours until the fruit is tender when prodded with a skewer. Loosen the sides of the cake with a knife and carefully push out the cake.

Dust very generously with icing sugar and serve either warm or cold with cream. Keep covered in the refrigerator and eat within 4 days.

# Turkey with Mushroom, Celery and Cranberry Sauce

Serves 4

*Turkey roasts can be rather bland and are greatly improved by the addition of such a delicious sauce as this.*

1¼ lb (550 g) turkey breast roast

*Sauce:*
1 oz (25 g) butter
2 onions, chopped
2 sticks celery, finely sliced
1 oz (25 g) flour
½ pint (300 ml) stock
4 oz (100 g) cranberries
4 oz (100 g) mushrooms,
   quartered
salt and pepper
1 level tablespoon caster sugar
   (optional)

Heat the oven to 350 °F, 180 °C, gas mark 4. Cook the turkey roast as directed on the wrapper.

Meanwhile make the sauce: melt the butter in a saucepan, add the onions and celery, cover the pan and cook gently for 10 minutes. Stir in the flour and cook for 1 minute. Add the stock and bring to the boil, stirring until thick. Add the cranberries, mushrooms, salt and pepper, and simmer gently for about 15 minutes or until the cranberries are tender. Taste and check seasoning and, if liked, add a little sugar.

Cut the turkey roast into slices and arrange on a warm serving dish. Spoon the sauce over and serve.

# Currant

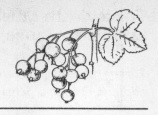

Currants, black, white and red, are among the most useful of the soft fruits.

**Black currants** are small purple-black berries with a fairly tough skin and a juicy, slightly acid flesh. Their season is July and August. Many soft-fruit growers offer them for sale on a pick-your-own basis, as the cost of harvesting is now very high. Greengrocers usually sell them stripped from their stalks. When you buy, look for firm, clean and glossy fruit, avoiding any that look withered or dusty. If yours are on the stalk it is easy enough to strip them by running the stalk gently through the prongs of a fork.

Black currants can be used as pudding and pie fillings and they make excellent jams and jellies, and fruit drinks that are particularly soothing to sore throats.

They can be bought ready-frozen to store in your freezer. To freeze your own, choose only those that are just ripe. Top and tail them, spread them on trays and freeze. Then put them into strong polythene bags when they have frozen individually. They will keep in the freezer for up to one year.

**Red currants** have the same season and the same form of growth as black, but the colour is a jewel-bright translucent red. They have a very distinctive flavour. They are always sold on the stalks and must be stripped, using the prongs of a fork. They are served fresh as a dessert or added to fruit salad. They make an excellent jelly which is served with roast lamb, venison, jugged hare. Freeze as black currants.

**White currants** are used as dessert fruit, stripped from their stalks and served with plenty of sugar.

**Black currant recipes:**

Other recipes using black currants:

Red currant recipe:

Recipe also using red currants:

See also:

White currant recipe, see:

# Black Currant Fool

Serves 4

*If you mix in the cream very slowly and lightly, you will have a lovely-looking fool, streaked with cream.*

1 lb (450 g) black currants
¼ pint (150 ml) water

5 oz (150 g) caster sugar
¼ pint (150 ml) double cream

Strip the black currants from their stalks, using a fork.

Place the water and sugar in a saucepan and stir over a gentle heat until the sugar has dissolved. Then add the black currants and simmer gently for about 10 minutes or until soft. Sieve the currants into a bowl and leave them to become quite cold.

Pour the fruit purée into a serving dish. Lightly whisk the cream until it begins to thicken but is not so thick that it will hold a soft peak. Spoon the cream into the purée, stirring slowly so that the cream makes streaks but is not mixed in.

## Black Currant Drink

You can make your own black currant drink. Stew the fruit until it is tender; 1 lb (450 g) fruit to ½ pint (300 ml) water. Then sieve it and add sugar to taste; if you intend to dilute the purée as a drink, add 1 lb (450 g) sugar to that amount of fruit. Store in the refrigerator and dilute with water to taste.

# Fresh Black Currant Sauce

*This sauce will keep in the refrigerator for up to 3 days. Reheat before serving.*

8 oz (225 g) black currants
7 fl oz (210 ml) water

3 oz (75 g) granulated sugar
2 level teaspoons cornflour

Strip the black currants from their stalks.

Place the water and sugar in a small saucepan and stir over a gentle heat until the sugar has dissolved. Then add the black currants and simmer gently for 10 minutes until they are soft.

Sieve the currants into a bowl to make a thin purée. Rinse out the saucepan, add the cornflour and mix to a paste with a little cold water and then stir in the fruit purée. Return to the heat and bring to the boil, stirring until thickened. Simmer for a minute or two. Taste, and, if necessary, a little extra sugar may be added to sweeten.

Turn into a jug or bowl and leave to cool. Serve hot or cold with ice cream. In winter this sauce is delicious served hot with a sponge pudding.

## Red Currant Sauce

Make as Fresh Black Currant Sauce above and serve cold with ice cream or poached pears, apricots or peaches.

## Black Currant Griestorte                Serves 8

*A beautifully textured almond sponge that also goes very well with red currants. If you have both kinds of currants, use a combination.*

3 eggs, separated
4 oz (100 g) caster sugar
½ teaspoon almond essence
2 oz (50 g) ground semolina
½ oz (12.5 g) ground almonds

*Filling:*
6 oz (175 g) black currants
3 oz (75 g) caster sugar
2 tablespoons water
1 level teaspoon cornflour
¼ pint (150 ml) whipping cream

Heat the oven to 350 °F, 180 °C, gas mark 4. Line an 8 inch (20 cm) cake tin with greased greaseproof paper and dust with flour.

Put the egg yolks and caster sugar in a heat-proof bowl over a pan of hot water and whisk until the mixture is pale and thick. Remove from the heat and fold in the almond essence, semolina and ground almonds. Whisk the egg whites until they form soft peaks, then fold into the mixture.

Turn into the cake tin and bake in the oven for 30 minutes or until the cake is well risen and pale golden. Turn the cake out and leave to cool on a wire rack. When it is quite cool, carefully split the cake in half.

Meanwhile strip the black currants from the stalks and place them with the sugar and water in a saucepan and cook very gently until the black currants are tender. Blend the cornflour with a teaspoon of cold water and stir into the black currants. Cook gently for 2 to 3 minutes until the mixture is thick. Remove the pan from the heat and leave the fruit to cool.

Whisk the cream until just thick and spread it over the bottom of the cake. Cover the cream with the black currant mixture and then top with the other piece of cake. Place on a serving dish and keep cool until required. Dust with icing sugar when ready to serve.

# Damson

The damson is a type of plum, smaller and dark-blue to black in colour, with yellow flesh. The fruit is sour unless very ripe and should be used only for cooking and jam-making. To cook, remove stalks and stew the fruit with plenty of sugar, either whole or halved with the stones removed. Freeze in strong polythene bags.

## Damson Syllabub

Serves 6 to 8

*This syllabub has a beautiful deep-red colour.*

1 lb (450 g) damsons or plums
4 oz (100 g) caster sugar
¼ pint (150 ml) water

2 egg whites
½ pint (300 ml) double cream

Wash the damsons. Place the sugar in a saucepan with the water and stir over a gentle heat until the sugar has dissolved. Then add the damsons, cover and simmer gently until soft.

Sieve into a large bowl and discard the stones. Leave the fruit purée to become quite cold. Lift out 2 tablespoons of the purée and keep on one side.

Whisk the egg whites until they are stiff but not dry and then whisk the cream until it forms soft peaks. Fold the cream into the purée and lastly fold in the egg whites. Turn the syllabub into a glass serving dish or divide it between 6 to 8 stemmed glasses and, using a teaspoon, trail a little of the reserved purée over the top. Chill for 3 hours.

# Date

Fresh dates are plumb and shiny, the skins smooooth and yellow-red to golden-brown in colour. They are available from October to February. More familiar, sweeter and stickier, are dried dates, packed in boxes of traditional shape – rounded ends, a camel or a pyramid on the outside, lined with lacy paper inside and provided with a long fork for extracting the fruit. These are eaten as dessert, often with nuts. Second quality dates are sold stoned and pressed into blocks to be used for cooking. Use them in puddings or for baking – for date and walnut loaf, for example. The best dates come from Israel. Fresh dates will keep in the refrigerator if wrapped, for three days. Freeze in strong polythene bags.

**Recipes:**
Fresh Date, Apple and Walnut
   Salad, 71
Date and Apricot Cheesecake, 72
Date and Walnut Cake, 73
Fresh Date Slices, 74

No-Cook Chutney, 74

**Recipe also using dates:**
Rhubarb and Apple Chutney,
   162

## Fresh Date, Apple and Walnut Salad          Serves 4

*Make this salad several hours ahead so that the rice takes on the flavour of the dates and dressing.*

4 oz (100 g) long-grain rice
8 oz (225 g) fresh dates
2 oz (50 g) shelled walnuts
2 medium-sized dessert apples
4 tablespoons oil

2 tablespoons vinegar
2 tablespoons lemon juice
1 level teaspoon dry mustard
salt and pepper

Cook the rice in plenty of boiling salted water until just tender; this usually takes about 10 to 12 minutes, or follow the directions on the packet. Rinse in warm water and drain very thoroughly.

Cut the dates in half, remove the stones, then roughly chop the flesh. Chop the walnuts and add to the dates.

Core and slice the apples, putting them in a bowl of salted water to prevent discolouration.

Put the oil, vinegar, lemon juice, mustard and a little seasoning in a bowl and whisk until blended.

Drain the apples and add them to the date mixture, together with the rice. Add the dressing and mix thoroughly; it is important that the apples are coated with the dressing. Taste, check seasoning and then serve with cold meats or slices of cheese.

# Date and Apricot Cheesecake                    Serves 8

*This cheesecake is quickest made with canned apricots. Fresh apricots can be used if liked but you will need to poach them for a few minutes first.*

1 lb (450 g) fresh dates
4 oz (100 g) butter
8 oz (225 g) gingernut biscuit
   crumbs, crushed
¼ teaspoon cinnamon
15½ oz (439 g) can apricot
   halves, drained
1½ packets or ¾ oz (20 g) gelatine
2 tablespoons lemon juice
2 eggs, separated
2 oz (50 g) caster sugar
¼ pint (150 ml) whipping cream
8 oz (225 g) rich cream cheese

*To decorate:*
¼ pint (150 ml) whipping cream

Oil the base and sides of an 8 inch (20 cm) loose-bottomed or spring-form cake tin.

Halve the dates lengthways and remove the stones. Arrange about half the dates, cut sides down, over the base of the tin.

Melt the butter, then add biscuit crumbs and cinnamon and stir well. Spoon this mixture over the dates and smooth flat. Chop the drained apricots finely and spread half the amount over the crumb mixture with another 6 to 8 dates. Purée the remaining apricots to make a sauce and set on one side.

Place the gelatine and lemon juice in a small bowl or cup and leave for a few minutes until it becomes sponge-like. Stand the bowl or cup in a pan of gently simmering water until the gelatine has dissolved and become quite clear.

Whisk the egg whites until stiff, and then whisk in the caster sugar, a teaspoonful at a time, until the meringue is very stiff.

Whisk the cream until it forms soft peaks.

Beat the egg yolks with the softened cream cheese and stir in the gelatine. Fold in the egg whites and cream and pour into the tin. Chill in the refrigerator for at least three hours, longer if possible.

Turn the cheesecake out of the tin and place on a serving dish. Spoon the prepared apricot sauce around the edge of the cheesecake.

Decorate the cheesecake with the remaining halved dates, placing them with cut sides alternately up and down. Whisk more cream until stiff and pipe in rosettes over the top.

## Date and Walnut Cake

*Fresh dates are less sweet than dried dates and go particularly well with nuts.*

8 oz (225 g) self-raising flour
4 oz (100 g) margarine
4 oz (100 g) demerara sugar
1 level teaspoon mixed spice

8 oz (225 g) fresh dates, stoned
 and chopped
2 oz (50 g) walnuts, chopped
5 tablespoons milk
1 egg, lightly beaten

Heat the oven to 325°F, 160°C, gas mark 3. Grease and line with greased greaseproof paper a 2 lb (900 g) loaf tin.

Put the flour in a bowl, add the margarine cut into small pieces and rub in with the fingertips until the mixture resembles fine breadcrumbs. Add the sugar and spice and stir in the dates and nuts. Mix the milk with the egg and blend with the dry ingredients.

Turn the mixture into the loaf tin and bake in the oven for about 1½ to 1¾ hours, or until a warm skewer inserted in the centre comes out clean.

Leave to cool in the tin, then turn out, remove paper and store in an airtight container.

# Fresh Date Slices

Makes 12 to 16 slices

*These can be served warm, with a dollop of cream on top, as a pudding.*

5 oz (150 g) plain flour
1 level teaspoon baking
  powder
1 level teaspoon cocoa
5 oz (150 g) light soft brown
  sugar
6 oz (175 g) fresh dates, stoned,
  skinned and chopped
4 oz (100 g) butter, melted
1 egg, beaten
a few drops of vanilla essence

*Icing:*
4 oz (100 g) icing sugar
1 level tablespoon cocoa
water to mix

Heat the oven to 350 °F, 180 °C, gas mark 4. Grease an 11 by 7 by 1 inch (27.5 by 17.5 by 2.5 cm) tin.

Sieve the flour, baking powder and cocoa into a bowl and stir in the sugar and dates. Add the melted butter, egg and vanilla essence and mix thoroughly. Turn into the tin, spread flat and bake for 30 minutes in the oven. Remove and leave in the tin.

For the icing, sieve the icing sugar together with the cocoa into a bowl and stir in sufficient water to give a coating consistency. Pour the icing over the cake while it is still warm and then leave to become quite cold.

Cut into fingers and then lift out and store in an airtight tin.

# No-Cook Chutney

Makes 3 lb (1.4 kg)

*If you have a rather warm kitchen do keep this chutney in the refrigerator.*

8 oz (225 g) stoneless dates
8 oz (225 g) sultanas
8 oz (225 g) onions
8 oz (225 g) apples, weighed
  after peeling and coring
8 oz (225 g) soft brown sugar

½ pint (300 ml) malt vinegar
½ level teaspoon salt
ground black pepper
pinch cayenne pepper
¼ level teaspoon ground ginger
1 level teaspoon pickling spice

Mince the dates, sultanas, onions and apples into a large bowl, using a coarse blade on the mincer. Stir in the sugar and vinegar and mix well.

Add the salt, black pepper, cayenne and ground ginger. Put the pickling spice in a small square of butter muslin and tie it loosely with a piece of string. Put this into the bowl and stir. Then cover and leave in a cool place for 24 hours, stirring occasionally.

Remove the bag from the chutney and put into clean, dry jars and cover with vinegar-proof lids to seal.

This chutney may be eaten at once or will keep well for 6 months if stored in a cool dry place.

# Elderberry

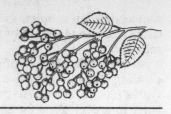

This is the fruit of the elder tree which grows wild in country hedgerows. The berries grow in bunches, are nearly black in colour and ripen in late summer.

Ripe firm fruit should be picked while still on the stems. Strip the berries as you would currants. Wash the fruit gently in cold water and drain before use. The berries are best used the same day as they are picked, although they will keep for a couple of days in the refrigerator.

Elderberries are used almost exclusively to make wine, which has a well-deserved reputation for being a potent brew.

They can be frozen in strong polythene bags.

## Elderberry Cordial

Wash the elderberries and place them in a saucepan. Cover the fruit with water and stew until soft.

Strain the fruit through a jelly bag and to each pint (600 ml) of juice obtained add 1 lb (450 g) granulated sugar. Stir until the sugar is dissolved.

Put the liquid into warm bottles, seal and leave to cool. When they are quite cold, store in the refrigerator for up to 6 weeks.

Serve diluted to taste with water or soda.

The juice may be frozen in plastic containers and keeps for up to 6 months.

# Fig

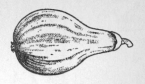

Fresh figs are imported from the Mediterranean countries. The fruit is pear-shaped, soft to the touch and the skin is white, red or purple. The deep-red flesh is very juicy and full of seeds. The skin can be removed by putting the fruit in hot water and then peeling it off.

Fresh figs are available from August to December. Use them as a dessert fruit. Most figs grown in Britain do not ripen properly every year and are best stewed in the same manner as pears.

Figs are also sold dried and these can be eaten raw. You can also buy them dried and pressed into blocks for cooking purposes; the flavour is improved by first soaking them in water for 24 hours.

Fresh figs can be frozen. Choose good-quality fruit, with no signs of bruising. Freeze the figs whole or halved, in strong polythene bags, or peel them and pack in cold sugar syrup.

**Fig recipe, see:**
Green Fruit Salad, 27

# Gooseberry

There is a good selection of gooseberries to choose from. Round or long, hairy or smooth, dessert or culinary, they come in different colours too – green, yellow, red. Generally speaking, smaller greener, sourer gooseberries are for cooking; yellow ones are large and sweet and best for eating raw; and red can be either, depending on how ripe they are. The season is May to July. Make sure they are free from blemishes or dirt. Dessert berries should be ripe but not squashy.

To prepare the berries, remove the tops and tails with kitchen scissors or with a sharp knife. Discard damaged fruit and, if it is dirty, wash and drain thoroughly. If you are not using the berries at once, spread them out on a dish; do not leave them piled in a basin or the fruit will soon turn mouldy.

Gooseberries can be frozen in strong polythene bags.

Recipes:

## Mackerel Stuffed with Gooseberries

*Mackerel and a piquant gooseberry purée make an excellent combination.*

gooseberries
salt and pepper

sugar
1 mackerel per person

Stew the gooseberries with a minimal amount of water, until

reduced to a thick purée. Season generously with salt, pepper and sugar, allow up to 2 oz (50 g) sugar to 8 oz (225 g) fruit.

Fillet the fish and open them flat. Spread the purée on one side, then press the fish together and lay in a buttered ovenproof dish.

Bake at 350 °F, 180 °C, gas mark 4, for about 30 minutes until the fish are cooked.

# Gooseberry Cloud
Serves 4

*When gooseberries are not in season this sweet may be made with plums or apricots. For children, instead of combining the purée with a custard, try mixing it with slightly softened vanilla ice cream.*

| Purée: | Custard: |
|---|---|
| 1 lb (450 g) gooseberries | 3 eggs |
| 4 tablespoons water | 1 oz (25 g) caster sugar |
| 4 oz (100 g) granulated sugar | ½ pint (300 ml) milk |

Remove the tops and tails from the gooseberries. Wash the fruit and place it in a saucepan with the water and sugar. Bring to the boil, stirring occasionally, then cover and simmer for 15 minutes until the fruit is soft and mushy. Sieve into a bowl and leave on one side to cool.

Make the custard: separate 2 of the eggs, putting the yolks in a small bowl and the whites in a larger bowl. Add the whole egg to the yolks, together with the sugar and milk and blend well. Pour into a saucepan and cook over a very low heat, stirring until the mixture thickens and coats the back of the spoon. Do not allow the custard to boil. Remove from the heat, pour into a basin and leave to cool. Cover the surface with a piece of damp greaseproof paper to stop a skin forming.

Stir half of the gooseberry purée into the cold custard. If liked, add a little green colouring. Divide the mixture between 4 individual glasses.

Whisk the egg whites until they are stiff and fold in the remaining gooseberry purée. Pile on top of the dishes and serve. This sweet is good served with brandy snaps.

# Gooseberry Cheesecake

Serves 8

*Use green gooseberries for this recipe – they give a delicious flavour and a bright green colour to the cheesecake filling.*

| | |
|---|---|
| 1 lb (450 g) gooseberries | 8 oz (225 g) rich cream cheese |
| 1 tablespoon ginger syrup from a jar of stem ginger | ¼ pint (150 ml) soured cream |
| | 2 eggs, separated |
| 4 oz (100 g) caster sugar | 2 oz (50 g) butter |
| 3 tablespoons water | 2 oz (50 g) ginger biscuits |
| ½ oz (12.5 g) gelatine | 2 oz (50 g) digestive biscuits |

Line an 8 inch (20 cm) cake tin with a circle of greaseproof paper.

Top and tail the gooseberries and place them in a saucepan with the ginger syrup and sugar. Simmer over a low heat until the gooseberries are tender. Do not rush this stage; let them cook slowly for 15 to 20 minutes until the juice runs out and a thick purée is obtained. Stir frequently.

Put the water in a small bowl or cup and sprinkle the gelatine over; leave to soak for 5 minutes. Remove the pan from the heat and stir in the soaked gelatine until it has dissolved. Put the gooseberries in a blender and purée until smooth and then sieve to remove all the pips. Turn into a bowl and leave to cool, stirring occasionally until the mixture starts to set. Cream the cheese and soured cream together and beat in the egg yolks and gooseberry purée. Whisk the egg whites until they are stiff and then fold them into the fruit mixture.

Turn the mixture into the tin and leave in the refrigerator until set.

Melt the butter in a small saucepan. Crush the biscuits finely and stir into the melted butter. Spread over the cheesecake and return to the refrigerator to chill for at least another hour.

Reverse the cheesecake onto a flat serving dish so that the crust is underneath. Remove the greaseproof paper. If liked, decorate the top with swirls of cream and tiny pieces of stem ginger.

# Bottled Gooseberries with Elderflowers

Makes about 12 lb (6 kg)

*Gooseberries bottled with a flavoured syrup can be opened and served at once.*

9 to 11 lb (4 to 5 kg) gooseberries
3 handfuls of elderflowers

4 pints (2.3 litres) boiling water
1¾ lb (800 g) granulated sugar

Wash the gooseberries. Top and tail them using a knife so that a little of the gooseberry skin is taken off. This saves pricking them to prevent shrivelling.

Pack the fruit tightly into jars. If there is a wide variety in size of fruit, grade by packing smallest and largest fruits in separate jars.

Place the elderflowers in a saucepan. Pour on the boiling water. Cover and leave to infuse for 15 minutes. Strain off the liquid and discard the elderflowers. Return the liquid to the saucepan with the sugar and bring to the boil, stirring continually until the sugar has dissolved. Quickly fill warmed jars to within ½ inch (1.25 cm) of the top. Place lids on jars. Rest screw-tops in place but *do not screw down* – the contents will expand.

Stand the jars in a large roasting tin containing 1 inch (2.5 cm) of hot water. Place on a low shelf in the oven at 300 °F, 150 °C, gas mark 2, until bubbles rise in the jars, the gooseberries change colour from green to greeny-yellow and the fruit shrinks slightly and rises about ½ inch (1.25 cm) from the bottoms of the jars. This will take about 1½ to 2 hours.

Remove the jars carefully from the oven, one at a time, and at once screw down each lid very tightly. Wipe the outsides of the jars with a warm damp cloth to remove any syrup. Leave to cool and then store until required.

# Grape

Most grapes grown in this country are produced in hot houses, but they *can* flourish in the open on a sunny wall. A small Oxfordshire town has a vine growing up the front of, appropriately, the local wine merchant's shop, bearing bunches of grapes at the proper season. But most grapes on sale in Britain are imported and there is a good supply of them all the year round, at varying prices.

Grapes can be black or white, that is purple or green. Black are usually the more expensive, although there is a reddish kind that is cheaper. The best white grapes have a distinctive Muscat flavour. Bunches of small, sweet, seedless, white grapes are available at certain seasons. Dessert grapes have a delicate bloom on the skin, which means that they must be carefully handled and not washed before serving.

Grapes are rarely cooked but are eaten simply as dessert fruit or added to fruit salad or used as decoration for sweets, jellies, cakes and trifles. Seedless grapes can be frozen whole, others should be peeled, halved and pipped. Pack in cold syrup.

# Glazed Fruit Flan

Serves 8

*Ensure that the fruits you choose combine well and balance each other in flavour and colour.*

**Pastry:**
4 oz (100 g) butter
2 oz (50 g) caster sugar
1 egg, beaten
1 egg yolk
8 oz (225 g) plain flour

**Glaze:**
6 rounded tablespoons apricot
  jam
4 tablespoons water

**Filling:**
a selection of fruits in season
  e.g. black and white grapes,
  bananas, apricots,
  strawberries

Prepare the pastry: cream the butter until it is soft, add the sugar and mix well. Add the egg and yolk a little at a time, stirring just sufficiently to blend it into the mixture. Finally stir in the flour and, with your hands, blend to a smooth paste. Wrap in foil and chill for 30 minutes.

Heat the oven to 400 °F, 200 °C, gas mark 6.

Roll out the pastry on a floured table to a rectangle large enough to line a Swiss roll tin 13 by 9 inches (32.5 by 22.5 cm). Press firmly against the base and sides of the tin and prick with a fork. Return to the refrigerator for a further 15 minutes. Line the flan case with greaseproof paper, fill with a layer of baking beans and bake in the oven for 25 minutes. Remove paper and beans and bake for a further 5 to 10 minutes until pastry is golden brown. Remove the flan case from the oven and leave to cool in the tin.

When cold, arrange rows of fruit in the flan.

Sieve the jam into a small saucepan, add water and stir to blend. Then simmer for a minute or two, until it becomes thick and syrupy. Using a pastry brush, coat the fruit with hot glaze, then allow to become quite cold before cutting.

# Plaice Veronique

Serves 4

*A classic French dish, usually made with Dover soles.*

| | |
|---|---|
| 4 large plaice fillets | ¼ (150 ml) dry cider |
| butter | 1½ level tablespoons cornflour |
| salt and pepper | ¼ pint (150 ml) milk |
| juice of half a lemon | 4 oz (100 g) green grapes |

Well butter a large frying pan. Fold the fillets in half, skin side innermost, and lay them in the pan. Dot with butter and season well. Cover with a tightly-fitting lid or a piece of foil and cook the fish gently over a low heat until tender. This will take about 10 to 15 minutes.

Carefully lift the fish from the pan, arrange them on a warm serving dish and keep them warm.

Add the cider to the pan. Blend the cornflour with the milk and add it to the pan. Bring to the boil, stirring until the sauce has thickened.

Halve the grapes and remove the pips. Add the grapes to the sauce and simmer for 2 minutes. Then taste, check seasoning and spoon over the fish.

# Grape and Lemon Cream

Serves 4

*This is an unusually sharp cream that is set in individual glasses or dishes and then topped by a grape and cream curd mixture.*

| | |
|---|---|
| 2 level teaspoons powdered gelatine | ¼ pint (150 ml) double cream |
| 2 tablespoons water | finely grated rind and juice of half a lemon |
| 15.9 oz (450 g) carton natural yogurt | |
| 8 oz (225 g) black grapes | |
| 2 level tablespoons lemon curd | |

Sprinkle the gelatine on the water in a small cup and place the cup in a saucepan filled with a little water and heat gently until the gelatine has dissolved. Leave to cool.

Lightly whisk the yoghurt and stir in the gelatine. Leave in a cool place until it starts to set.

Whisk the cream until it just forms soft peaks and add the grated lemon rind and half the lemon juice, whisking in carefully.

Fold into the yogurt and divide between 4 sundae glasses or individual dishes and chill in the refrigerator.

Just before serving, halve the grapes and remove the pips. Blend the lemon curd with the remaining lemon juice. Arrange the grapes on top of the yogurt and spoon the lemon glaze over the top.

# Grapefruit

Grapefruit is the largest of the citrus fruits imported from the warmer countries and is available all the year round. It is a round, squat fruit with pale-yellow skin and very juicy yellow flesh, and few or no pips. A pink-tinged variety with pink flesh is now coming to us from the United States.

When buying grapefruit, see that the skin has a shiny lustre and that there is no trace of brown at the stem point. A grapefruit that feels heavy will have plenty of juice inside.

Grapefruit is usually eaten raw, at breakfast or as a first course at dinner. It is considered by some slimmers to have almost magical qualities. It is used as the basis of fresh fruit drinks, in fruit salads, and it makes good marmalade, often with the addition of oranges. It is available canned and you can buy canned or frozen juice.

A special grapefruit knife is useful for preparing the fruit. It has a curved blade to help remove the segments from the cut grapefruit. Slip the knife blade between pith and flesh and between flesh and membrane. Loosen the flesh gently. Then cut through the membrane close to the skin and remove it whole, leaving the segments of flesh in the grapefruit shell. This is possible after a bit of practice.

Grapefruit keeps well. Store in a cool, well-ventilated place but do not put it in the refrigerator or the flesh will dry out. It can be frozen whole or divided into segments.

Recipes:
Citrus Fruit Salad, 87
Grapefruit and Orange Marmalade, 87
Chicory and Grapefuit Salad, 88
Hot Grapefruit, 88

# Citrus Fruit Salad

Serves 6

*Serve very cold with either whipped cream or a mixture of plain yogurt and whipped cream.*

2 grapefruit
3 oranges
1 lime, optional

2 satsumas
8 oz (225 g) caster sugar
3 tablespoons orange liqueur

Slice both ends from the grapefruit and oranges. Stand the oranges on a plate and slice through the skin, down and around the oranges, to remove all the peel and pith, leaving the peeled orange complete. Cut in between the membranes and remove the fruit in segments. Repeat with the grapefruit and the lime, if used.

Peel the satsumas and cut them across into slices.

Layer the fruit in a glass serving dish and sprinkle with the caster sugar as you go. Cover and leave to marinate in the refrigerator overnight.

Just before serving, stir in the orange liqueur.

# Grapefruit and Orange Marmalade

Makes about 10 lb (4.5 kg)

2 lb (900 g) Seville oranges
1 grapefruit
2 large lemons

6 pints (3.4 litres) water
6 lb (2.7 kg) granulated sugar

Wash the fruit, cut them in half and squeeze the juice out into a large saucepan. Pull away most of the pulp and pith from the inside of the fruit halves. Then quarter the peels and slice finely. Put the pulp, pith and pips into a piece of muslin and tie with string to form a bag. Put the shredded peel and the muslin bag into the saucepan with the juice. Bring to the boil and simmer without a lid. Cook gently for about 2 hours or until the peel feels quite tender and soft. Remove the muslin bag.

Add the sugar and dissolve over a low heat. Then bring to the boil and boil rapidly until setting point is reached. This will take approximately 25 to 30 minutes. (See Crab Apple Jelly, page 61.)

Draw the pan from the heat and skim. Then cool the marmalade and stir before potting in clean warm jars. Cover and label.

## Chicory and Grapefruit Salad                    Serves 6 to 8

*This salad goes very well with most cold meats, particularly tongue and brawn.*

5 large heads of chicory
2 large grapefruit
3 to 6 oz (75 to 175 g)
    demerara sugar
1 bunch watercress

*Dressing:*
6 tablespoons oil
2 tablespoons wine vinegar
¼ level teaspoon salt
¼ level teaspoon pepper
½ to 1 teaspoon caster sugar
½ teaspoon French mustard

Divide the chicory into leaves, then rinse in cold water and dry thoroughly. Peel the grapefruit so that all the peel and pith are removed (see Orange Salad, page 120). Cut the grapefruit into thin slices, remove any remaining pips and cut each slice in half.

Arrange the chicory leaves in the bottom and on each side of a long dish, then put layers of grapefruit slices in the centre of the dish, sprinkling each layer with demerara sugar. Finish with overlapping slices of grapefruit.

Just before serving, pour the prepared dressing over the salad and decorate with watercress.

## Hot Grapefruit                    Serves 4

*If you have the oven on anyway, put the grapefruit at the top of the oven, rather than under the grill, until the sugar has melted and the grapefruit has heated through. A spoonful of rum, if liked, can be poured over the top before serving.*

2 large grapefruit
4 tablespoons light soft brown
    sugar

½ level teaspoon ground
    cinnamon or ginger
large knob of butter

Cut the grapefruit in half and cut around each half to loosen the flesh. Cut between the segments and remove any pith and white skin. Mix the sugar with the spice and sprinkle over the grapefruit. Dot the halves with butter.

Place under a moderate grill and grill lightly until the sugar has melted and the grapefruit halves are hot through.

# Greengage

Greengages are a type of plum, small, round and greenish-yellow. They have a distinctive flavour of their own. They are grown in Britain much as their larger relatives the plums, and are also imported. The season is August and September.

They can be eaten as a dessert fruit, or cooked. They can be stewed whole or halved and the stones removed. They make very pleasant pies and tarts.

To freeze, either leave whole and put in strong polythene bags or halve, remove stones and pack in syrup in rigid containers.

**Recipes:**
Greengage Cobbler, 89
Iced Greengage Creams, 90

**See also:**
Crunchy Plum Betsie, 150
Plum and Almond Tart, 151

## Greengage Cobbler

Serves 4 to 6

*A cobbler is simply a scone mixture on top of fruit. Other fruits that can be used are plums, apples, blackberry and apple – in fact, any combination that you like.*

2 lb (900 g) greengages,
   washed, quartered and
   stoned
4 oz (100 g) granulated sugar

**Cobbler:**
8 oz (225 g) self-raising flour
2 oz (50 g) butter
2 oz (50 g) caster sugar
1 egg, beaten
3 to 4 tablespoons milk

Heat the oven to 425 °F, 220 °C, gas mark 7.

Put the greengages into a fairly shallow ovenproof dish and sprinkle over the sugar and put in the oven for 10 minutes.

Meanwhile make the cobbler: put the flour in a bowl, rub in the butter until the mixture resembles fine breadcrumbs. Then stir in the sugar, add the egg and milk and bind all the ingredients together to form a soft but not sticky dough. Roll out on a lightly floured surface to a thickness of ½ inch (1.25 cm) and, with a fluted 2 inch (5 cm) cutter, cut the dough into rounds.

Place these, slightly overlapping, around the edge of the dish. Brush the tops with a little milk and bake in the oven for a further 15 to 20 minutes, by which time the fruit will be tender and the scones well risen and golden brown.

# Iced Greengage Creams                                    Serves 6

*You can also use plums, damsons or particularly, young early rhubarb – but cook all these with less water than the greengages require.*

1½ lb (675 g) greengages  
¼ pint (150 ml) water  
6 oz (175 g) caster sugar  

½ pint (300 ml) double cream, lightly whipped  
3 egg whites

Put the greengages, water and sugar in a large saucepan, bring to the boil, stirring until the sugar has dissolved. Then cook gently until the greengages are soft and pulpy.

Pour into a large sieve and leave to drain. Reserve the juice, then put the sieve over another bowl and rub the greengages through to a purée. Leave to become quite cold. Fold in the cream.

Whisk the egg whites until they are stiff and then fold into the greengage purée.

Divide the mixture between 6 individual glasses and chill in the refrigerator.

Just before serving pour a little of the greengage syrup over each portion.

# Guava

The guava may be something of an acquired taste in this country. A tropical fruit, it is not easily come by in the local high street, but you can sometimes find it in West Indian shops or in specialist greengrocers. You can buy it bottled or canned.

The fresh fruit comes in various shapes and colours – sometimes pear-shaped, sometimes more like a tomato, some even like figs. The colour varies from yellow to crimson and there are a lot of seeds.

Guava can be eaten raw but it has a musky penetrating odour that those unaccustomed to it do not necessarily find attractive. Like the quince (quince recipes can be used for guava) it is best made into jelly or jam. Fresh guavas can be stewed or poached – cut the fruit into segments, remove the seeds and cook slowly with sugar in a little water.

For recipe using guavas, see Quince

# Japonica

The fruits of the ornamental japonica, the flowering quince, are in shape something like a cross between an apple and a pear. As they do not always ripen on the tree, they are often picked when green and stored until they turn yellow. The firm yellow-green flesh has a distinctive flavour, fairly sharp, and the fruit is at its best in October.

Japonica fruit is often mixed with apple for pies and tarts, and is commonly turned into delicious jam or jelly.

Recipes:                    Japonica Jam, 92
Japonica and Apple Pudding, 92   Japonica Jelly, 93

# Japonica and Apple Pudding

Serves 6

*Japonicas are harder than apples and, to peel, require a really sharp knife.*

6 oz (175 g) self-raising flour
2 oz (50 g) fresh white
  breadcrumbs
4 oz (100 g) shredded suet
10 tablespoons milk

4 oz (100 g) japonicas, peeled,
  cored and sliced
1 lb (450 g) cooking apples,
  peeled, cored and sliced
4 oz (100 g) soft brown sugar

Butter a 2 pint (1 litre) pudding basin. Put the flour, breadcrumbs and suet in a bowl. Add sufficient milk to make a soft dough and divide the mixture into three portions in graded sizes. Roll out the smallest portion to line the base of the basin.

Put the japonicas, apples and sugar in another basin and mix together and then put half the mixture in the basin on top of the dough.

Roll out the second portion of pastry to fit over the fruit. Put the remaining fruit on top and cover with the remaining rolled out to fit the basin.

Cover with a greased and pleated lid of greaseproof paper and a lid of foil. Steam or boil for about 3 hours. If boiling, place the bowl on an upturned saucer in a saucepan so that the boiling water comes halfway up the sides of the basin. In either case keep the water level topped up with boiling water during cooking.

Turn out on to a warm serving dish and serve with a custard sauce.

# Japonica Jam

Makes about 2½ lb (1.1 kg)

*This jam has a distinctive sharp flavour and is especially good with brown bread and butter.*

1 lb (450 g) japonicas
pinch of ground ginger
1¼ pints (750 ml) water

granulated sugar
juice of 2 lemons

Wash the japonicas but do not peel or core. Just cut them in half, add a good pinch of ground ginger, and simmer in the water until they are reduced to a pulp. Sieve the fruit and to each pint (600 ml) of pulp add 1 lb (450 g) granulated sugar and the lemon juice.

Put the fruit and sugar into a saucepan and bring to the boil, stirring until the sugar has dissolved. Then boil rapidly until setting point is reached. (See Crab Apple Jelly, page 61.)

Turn into clean warm jars, cover and label.

## Japonica Jelly

*This is delicious with cold meats and roast lamb.*

Wipe the fruit, but do not core or peel. Cut into pieces and put in a saucepan. And just sufficient water to cover the fruit and simmer it until it is soft and pulpy. Strain through a jelly bag overnight. To each pint (600 ml) of juice add 1 lb (450 g) granulated sugar. Put the juice and sugar in a saucepan, heat gently until the sugar has dissolved, bring to the boil and allow to boil rapidly until setting point is reached. (See Crab Apple Jelly, page 61.) Pot and seal as usual.

# Kiwi Fruit

Known also as Chinese gooseberries, these fruits are egg-shaped with a brownish-red skin covered with minute hairs. The soft, juicy, green flesh is pitted with black seeds. It has the richest vitamin C content of any fruit.

Most kiwi fruit is imported from New Zealand. The flavour has been described as watermelon with a hint of raspberry. When buying, avoid any fruit with shrivelled skins. The fruit is ready to eat when it is soft.

Serve peeled slices with a dash of lemon juice, or peel and add to fruit salad or use to decorate desserts. Use as a garnish for meat or fish. If rubbed over steak before grilling, the juice will tenderise the meat and give it a subtle flavour.

Recipe:

## Kiwi Fruit, Grape and Melon Salad

Serves 6 to 8

*Use either seedless grapes for this recipe, or really large green grapes and remove the pips.*

1 small honeydew melon, cut into cubes or balls
1½ lb (675 g) green grapes

3 kiwi fruits, peeled and sliced
4 .oz (100 g) caster sugar

Take a glass serving dish and layer the fruits in it, putting the melon in first. Then add the grapes and arrange the sliced kiwi fruits attractively on top. Sprinkle with sugar, cover and leave in the refrigerator to chill for about 8 hours.

Serve with plenty of lightly whipped cream or with lemon ice cream.

# Kumquat

Kumquat is a type of orange, about the size and shape of a plum. It is bright yellow with juicy, slightly bitter flesh and it came originally from China but is now grown in many parts of the world. We import it mainly from Morocco, but the fresh fruit is normally in very short supply. It is also canned, bottled, candied and made into marmalade.

The whole of the fruit is edible, even the rind, either raw or baked in syrup. It makes a good garnish for duck. Recipes for dishes using oranges can easily be adapted for kumquats. The resulting exotic flavour should baffle and intrigue your family and friends.

Look for a slight sheen on the skin of the fruit and a sweet aroma. Store in a cool, dry place (not the refrigerator), being careful not to damage the easily bruised skins.

**For recipes using kumquats, see Orange**

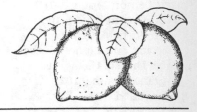

# Lemon

The lemon, unlike most other members of the great citrus family, is too acid to be eaten raw with any pleasure, but it is one of the most highly valued, and most used fruits in cookery. Imported from the Mediterranean countries and from South Africa, it is available all the year round.

Lemons vary very much in size and in thickness of the skin. Choose ones with a glossy skin and pick out those that feel heavy for their size because they will contain a lot of juice. The yellow rind, which contains the zest, the flesh and the juice are all used in cooking. Get the maximum juice out of a lemon by putting it in warm water for five minutes before squeezing. Alternatively, roll the fruit between the palms of your hands. Keep lemons in a cool place (not the refrigerator) and try to use them within four days of purchase. If you need only half a lemon, wrape the spare half in cling film and keep it for a couple of days in the refrigerator. Sprinkle cut fruit with lemon juice – apples, bananas, pears, avocados – to stop them discolouring. The empty shells or the juice are good for whitening your hands after washing up.

The uses of the lemon are virtually limitless. The rind and juice are used as flavourings in fruit sweets, cakes, puddings and pies – particularly lemon meringue pie. It makes fruit drinks and lemon curd, a tangy marmalade and sauce. It goes into savoury dishes and curries. Added to the water it helps to keep boiled rice fluffy. It also helps to set jam.

You can freeze whole lemons. Or squeeze the juice and freeze it in the ice-cube tray; remove the frozen cubes and store in polythene bags in the freezer.

# Lemon Meringue Pie                                    Serves 6

*This is delicious. For a change you can make this recipe using limes, but do not be tempted ever to use oranges; the flavour is not sufficiently sharp.*

**Pastry:**
6 oz (175 g) plain flour
2 oz (50 g) butter
2 oz (50 g) lard
1 egg yolk
½ oz (12.5 g) caster sugar
2 teaspoons cold water

*Lemon filling:*
2 large lemons
1½ oz (40 g) cornflour
½ pint (300 ml) water
2 egg yolks
3 oz (75 g) caster sugar

**Meringue topping:**
3 egg whites
4½ oz (125 g) caster sugar

First make the pastry: put the flour in a bowl, add the fats cut into small pieces and rub in with the fingertips until the mixture resembles fine breadcrumbs. Blend the egg yolk, sugar and water together and stir into the dry ingredients and bind them together. Roll out the pastry on a floured board and line a 9 inch (22.5 cm) flan tin. Chill in the refrigerator for 30 minutes.

Heat the oven, with a thick baking sheet in it, to 425 °F, 220 °C, gas mark 7. Line the flan with greaseproof paper and weigh down with baking beans and bake blind for 15 minutes.

Meanwhile prepare the filling: finely grate the rind and squeeze the juice from the lemons and place in a bowl with the cornflour, add 2 tablespoons water and blend to a smooth paste. Boil the remaining water and pour it on to the cornflour mixture. Return it to the pan, bring to the boil and simmer for 3 minutes until thick, stirring continuously. Remove from the heat and add the egg yolks blended with sugar. Return the pan to the heat for a moment to thicken the sauce and then cool slightly.

Remove the beans and greaseproof paper from the flan and spoon in the filling. Whisk the egg whites until they form stiff peaks, add the sugar a teaspoonful at a time, whisking well after each addition. Spoon the meringue over the lemon filling, being careful to spread it right up to the edge of the pastry, leaving no spaces.

Return the pie to the oven, reducing the heat to 325 °F, 160 °C, gas mark 3. Cook for about 30 minutes or until the pie is pale golden brown.

Serve the pie either warm or cold.

# Lemon Chicken

Serves 4

*A very simple recipe which really gives flavour to frozen chicken joints. If you have fresh lemon thyme in the garden, sprinkle a little over the top.*

4 chicken joints
4 oz (100 g) butter

freshly ground black pepper
grated rind and juice of 1 lemon

Heat the oven to 400 °F, 200 °C, gas mark 6.

Skin the chicken and lay the joints in a single layer in an ovenproof dish.

Put the butter, black pepper and lemon rind and juice in a bowl, cream well and then spread over the chicken. Bake in the oven for about 40 minutes or until the chicken is tender, basting frequently.

Serve from the dish with a little butter sauce spooned over each portion.

# Inexpensive Lemon Mousse

Serves 6

*Children enjoy this mousse. It will stretch to serve 8 if you make it in individual dishes.*

1 lemon jelly
½ pint (300 ml) boiling water
finely grated rind and juice of 2
  large or 3 small lemons

4 eggs, separated
2 to 4 oz (50 to 100 g) caster
  sugar
angelica

Put the jelly, broken into small pieces, into a large bowl. Add the boiling water and stir until the jelly has dissolved. Strain the lemon juice and stir, with the grated rind, into the jelly.

Beat the egg yolks with the caster sugar until they are creamy and stir into the jelly; leave in a cool place until the mixture starts to set.

Whisk the egg whites until they are stiff and then fold them into the lemon mixture. Turn into a 2½ pint (1.4 litre) glass serving dish and leave to set.

Decorate with small leaves of angelica.

# Lemon Pavlova with Kiwi Fruit          Serves 6 to 8

*The filling for this pavlova is very easy to make. It sounds rather rich and sickly, but it is not – the lemons add a saving sharpness. Other fruits you can try include small bunches of black and green grapes, fresh strawberries, raspberries, and red currants brushed with egg white and then dipped in caster sugar. It is a delicious-looking pudding.*

3 egg whites
6 oz (175 g) caster sugar
1 teaspoon vinegar
1 level teaspoon cornflour

*Filling:*
6 oz (196 g) can condensed
  milk
¼ pint (150 ml) double cream
juice of 2 large lemons

*Topping:*
2 kiwi fruit

Lay a sheet of silicone (non-stick vegetable parchment) on a baking tray and mark an 8 inch (20 cm) circle on it. Heat the oven to 325 °F, 160 °C, gas mark 3.

Whisk the egg whites until they are stiff and then whisk in the sugar a spoonful at a time. Blend the vinegar with the cornflour and whisk it, with the last spoonful of sugar, into the egg whites.

Spread the meringue out to cover the circle on the baking tray and build up the sides so that they are higher than the centre.

Put the baking tray in the centre of the oven, turn the heat down to 300 °F, 150 °C, gas mark 2 and bake the meringue for 1 hour. The pavlova will be a pale creamy colour rather than white. Turn the oven off but leave the pavlova in the oven to become quite cold.

Remove the pavlova from the baking tray and place on a serving dish.

Place the condensed milk, cream and lemon juice in a basin and beat until blended and the mixture is thick and creamy, then pile it into the centre of the pavlova. Place in the refrigerator and leave to stand for at least 1 hour before serving.

Peel and slice the kiwi fruit and arrange attractively around the edge of the lemon pavlova just before serving.

# Sharp Lemon Mousse                    Serves 6

*A very light, slimming mousse. If preferred, make it in 6 to 8 individual glasses. Leave off the cream if you are watching your figure. A very good Lime Mousse can be made the same way, but use 4 fresh limes instead of the lemons.*

4 eggs
4 oz (100 g) caster sugar
3 lemons
½ oz (12.5 g) gelatine

3 tablespoons cold water
whipped cream and lemon
   slices to decorate

Separate the eggs and place the yolks in a bowl with the sugar; beat until well-blended and creamy. Put the egg whites in a bowl ready for whisking. Grate the lemon rind and squeeze the juice from the lemons and add to the egg-yolk mixture.

Place the gelatine and water in a small bowl or cup. Stand for 3 minutes until it becomes sponge-like, then stand the bowl in a pan of simmering water and allow the gelatine to dissolve. Cool slightly and add it to the egg-yolk and lemon mixture. Leave to cool but not set.

Whisk the egg whites until they are stiff, then fold them into the lemon mixture. Turn into a 2 pint (a good litre) glass serving dish and leave in a cool place until set.

Decorate with whipped cream and small slices of lemon and serve at room temperature.

# Lemon Cream Sauce

*This is a very versatile sauce that may be served warm or cold. It is especially good with fish, with grilled lemon sole or plaice, herrings or mackerel and we like it with haddock. Serve it cold, as a change from tartar sauce, in a dollop on the side of the plate. A little lemon thyme or freshly chopped chives gives the sauce an extra tang.*

½ oz (12.5 g) butter
1 level tablespoon flour
¼ pint (150 ml) water
salt and pepper

thinly grated rind and juice of
   half a small lemon
1 egg yolk
¼ pint (150 ml) single cream

Melt the butter in a small saucepan and stir in the flour. Cook for 1 minute.

Gradually stir in the water, seasoning and lemon rind and juice. Bring to the boil, stirring until the sauce has thickened slightly.

Remove from the heat and stir in the egg yolk and cream. Then return to the heat and cook very gently but do not boil. Taste and check seasoning and serve either warm or cold.

# Lemon Sorbet

Serves 6

*If you like a slightly lighter mixture, you can add 3 egg whites, instead of 1, and serve it as a sherbert, which is rather softer than a sorbet. If you do this, leave it out of the refrigerator slightly longer before serving to give it time to soften.*

| | |
|---|---|
| 6 lemons | 6 oz (175 g) sugar |
| ½ pint (300 ml) water | 1 egg white |

Peel the rind thinly from 3 lemons and put in a saucepan with the water and sugar. Heat gently until the sugar has dissolved, then simmer for 10 minutes. Remove from the heat and leave to cool.

Cut the lemons in half and scoop out all the flesh, together with any juice, into a bowl. Remove the pips and then purée the flesh in the blender and sieve. Strain the sugar syrup on to the lemon purée and mix well. Turn into a rigid container, cover and freeze until half frozen.

Whisk the egg white until it is stiff. Turn the half-frozen lemon mixture into a bowl and whisk it until it is smooth. Fold in the egg white and then return to the container and freeze until firm. Cover and label.

When required leave the sorbet to soften slightly in the refrigerator for 15 minutes before serving, spooned into glasses.

# Tangerine and Lemon Sorbet

Make as for Lemon Sorbet but use 4 tangerines and 2 lemons, peeling the rind from all the tangerines and lemons and putting it in the saucepan with the water and sugar.

# Lemon Drizzle Cakes

Makes 12 drizzle cakes

*Top favourites in our family. If you prefer, make it in one large 8 inch (20 cm) cake tin, it will take about 50 minutes to cook.*

4 oz (100 g) soft margarine
1 level teaspoon baking powder
6 oz (175 g) self-raising flour
6 oz (175 g) caster sugar
2 eggs
4 tablespoons milk
finely grated rind of 1 lemon

*Icing:*
juice of 1 lemon
4 oz (100 g) caster sugar
3 level tablespoons lemon curd

Heat the oven to 350 °F, 180 °C, gas mark 4. Line a 11 by 7 by 1 inch (27.5 by 1.75 by 2.5 cm) tin with greased greaseproof paper.

Put the margarine, baking powder, flour, sugar, eggs, milk and lemon rind together in a large bowl and beat well for 1 minute. Turn the mixture into the tin and bake for about 20 minutes or until the cake has shrunk from the sides of the tin and springs back when pressed with a finger in the centre.

While the cake is baking, make the icing. Put the lemon juice, sugar and lemon curd in a small bowl and stir until blended.

When the sponge comes out of the oven, prick lightly all over with a fork and spread the lemon paste over the top while it is still hot. Leave in the tin until the cake is quite cold, then lift out, cut into slices and lift each slice off the paper with a palette knife.

# Hot Lemon Sauce

*To prevent a skin forming on the top of this sauce, you can put a piece of dampened greaseproof paper on the surface once it is made and keep it warm in the pan on the stove.*

grated rind and juice of 1 lemon
2 oz (50 g) caster sugar

1 oz (25 g) cornflour
½ pint (300 ml) water

Put the lemon rind and juice in a saucepan, together with the sugar and cornflour and then gradually stir in the water. Bring to the boil, stirring continuously until the sauce has thickened. Simmer for 2 minutes.

Serve hot with Fruit Fritters, Banana Rolls or on ice cream.

# Lemon Curd
Makes a good 1 lb (450 g)

*This is well worth making – both for home consumption and to give as a present. With tremendous care you can mix lemon curd without using a double saucepan, but do stir it constantly over a very low heat. Two tablespoons of home-made lemon curd mixed with ¼ pint (150 ml) whipped cream makes a very good, quick filling.*

grated rind and juice of 2
  lemons
2 oz (50 g) butter

2 large eggs
8 oz (225 g) caster sugar

Place all the ingredients in the top of a double saucepan with simmering water in the lower part. If you do not have a double saucepan, use a basin over a pan of water.

Stir well until the butter has melted and the sugar dissolved. Continue to stir over the simmering water until the curd thickens – this will take about 20 minutes so make sure that the curd is really thick.

Remove the pan from the heat and pour the lemon curd into clean warm jars. Cover and seal while still warm and then label.

Keep in a cool larder for a month or a refrigerator for about 3 months.

# Still Lemonade
Makes 10 to 12 glasses

*Old-fashioned lemonade is lovely to have in the refrigerator on warm summer days. Serve it with a sprig of fresh mint or a little blue-flowered borage in each glass.*

4 large lemons
4 oz (100 g) caster sugar

2 pints (a good litre) boiling
  water

Wipe the lemons and take off the peel very thinly with a potato peeler. Then squeeze the juice from the lemons and put in a small covered container in the refrigerator.

Put the lemon peel in a large bowl with the sugar. Pour over the boiling water, stir well, cover, leave to cool and then store in the refrigerator overnight.

Next day add the reserved lemon juice, mix well and strain into a jug.

# Lime

The lime is similar to a small lemon in shape, with a green skin and a sharp flavour. Fresh limes can be bought all the year round in this country, imported mainly from South Africa and the West Indies. Use them when they are still slightly unripe. Freeze and store in the same way as lemons.

In cooking, too, treat limes very much as lemons. They are much used in curries, and they bring a fresh new taste to drinks.

Lime recipe, see:
Citrus Fruit Salad, 87

See also:
Tangerine Syllabub, 169

For other recipes using limes,
  see Lemon

# Loganberry

The loganberry is a soft fruit similar to a raspberry but rather larger and darker in colour. It has a hard hull or core which is not easy to remove. If you do not care for this, sieve the berries before serving.

Loganberries grow on canes like raspberries. They are in season from June to August. When buying, pick out berries that are firm and dry and faintly shiny. Avoid punnets with a lot of fruit stains on them.

The fruit may be eaten raw, preferably with sugar as the flavour is a little sharp. Use in pies, puddings and tarts, or stew the fruit gently in a little water for about 10 minutes until the berries are soft but not broken up.

Whole berries can be open frozen on a tray until firm, then covered and labelled. Alternatively, freeze the fruit as a purée.

**Recipes:**
Fresh Loganberry Mousse, 105
Compôte of Loganberries and Apples, 106
Loganberry and Melon Salad, 106

**See also:**
Blackberry Shortcake, 52
Eve's Pudding, 23
Raspberry Queen of Puddings, 157

**Other recipes using loganberries:**
Loganberry Ice Cream, 191
Summer Pudding, 160

# Fresh Loganberry Mousse

Serves 4 to 6

*This mousse may also be made using blackberries and, because loganberries and blackberries freeze so well, can successfully be made out of season.*

1 lb (450 g) loganberries
4 oz (100 g) caster sugar
½ oz (12.5 g) gelatine

4 tablespoons water
½ pint (300 ml) whipping cream

Lay the loganberries in a single layer on a large flat dish. Sprinkle sugar over them and leave for at least 3 hours to allow the juice to run out; then sieve them. If you put the loganberries in a blender and purée until smooth before sieving, this speeds up the process and makes it easier.

Put the gelatine and water in a cup or small bowl and leave it to stand for 5 minutes until it becomes sponge-like. Stand the cup in a pan of simmering water until the gelatine is clear, remove from the heat, cool slightly and stir into the loganberry purée. Leave it until the purée starts to thicken and set.

Whisk the cream until it forms soft peaks and then fold it into the purée.

Turn the mixture into a glass serving dish, about 2 pint (1 litre) size, and leave to set.

# Compôte of Loganberries and Apples

Serves 4 to 6

*Any leftovers of this dish make a delicious addition to a raspberry or blackberry jelly.*

3 oz (75 g) caster sugar
3 tablespoons lemon juice
3 crisp eating apples

¼ level teaspoon cinnamon
12 oz (350 g) loganberries

Place the sugar in a large saucepan, together with the lemon juice, and dissolve it over a gentle heat.

Peel, core and thinly slice the apples straight into the saucepan, add the cinnamon and loganberries and leave over a low heat until the fruit begins to fall and the juice runs out.

Turn into a serving dish, cool and then chill for several hours. Serve with vanilla ice cream.

# Loganberry and Melon Salad

Serves 8

*If you do not have loganberries, this salad is equally delicious made with raspberries.*

1 lb (450 g) fresh loganberries
2 to 4 oz (50 to 100 g) caster
   sugar

2 to 3 tablespoons Grand
   Marnier or Kirsch
1 ripe melon about 2 lb (900 g)
   in weight

Put the loganberries into a bowl and sprinkle them with sugar, then pour the liqueur over. Cover and leave in a cool place for at least 1 hour so that the loganberries become juicy.

Cut the melon in half, remove the seeds, scoop out the flesh and cut it into small cubes. Add the melon to the loganberries, mix well and chill.

Turn the salad into a glass serving dish and serve with a bowl of whipped cream.

# Loquat

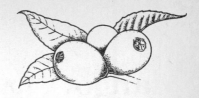

Loquat, or Japanese medlar, is a stone fruit similar to a plum with a smooth yellow skin. The juicy flesh is slightly tart. Loquats are imported from Israel all the year round but they are scarce in the shops. However, they are well worth seeking out if you want to serve something unusual.

Loquats can be eaten fresh or made into preserves. Choose firm fruit without blemishes. The fruit can be stewed whole or halved with stones removed. For fruit salad, remove the stones.

# Lychee

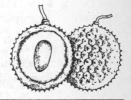

Lychee (or litchis) are of Chinese origin but are grown in many tropical countries. The main season is December to February. The stone fruits are the size of large cherries, oval-shaped, with hard scaly skins and a white pulpy flesh, and they have a distinctive flavour that is acid and sweet at the same time. They are eaten fresh, in fruit salads or in preserves. Canned lychees make a good substitute when fresh ones are not available. Lychees are sometimes dried and are then known as lychee nuts.

To peel a lychee, squeeze the fruit until the brittle shell cracks, then lift off the shell piece by piece. Squeeze out the stone. Use within three days of purchase.

**Lychee recipe, see:**
Green Fruit Salad, 27

# Mango

This tropical fruit varies a great deal in size. It may be as small as a plum or as much as 5 lb (2.2 kg) in weight. The colour of the smooth, tough skin varies from green to yellow-orange when really ripe. The yellowish flesh is smooth and soft, full of juice and with a delicate fragrance and spicy taste. Mangoes flourish in the warmer countries of the world and are commercially grown in India, China, Australia and the United States. They are available in Britain from January to September.

When choosing fresh mangoes, avoid any that are blemished or wrinkled. The flesh at the stalk should give to gentle pressure but not be too soft. Fresh mangoes are served as dessert fruits or as a garnish. To prepare them, score the skin with a sharp knife downwards from the non-stalk end into 1 inch (2.5 cm) sections. Then pull the skin downwards in strips as though peeling a banana. Slice the fruit, cutting right to the stone, and sprinkle with lemon juice. Eat either with or without sugar.

Green mangoes are used for chutneys and pickles.

Dried mango and powdered mango for flavouring dishes can be bought from Indian shops.

The ripe fruit can be frozen, peeled and sliced in syrup.

Recipe:
Sweet Mango Chutney, 109

Recipe also using mangoes:
Fruit Fritters, 26

# Sweet Mango Chutney

Makes about 4 lb (1.8 kg)

*Unless you have a cheap supply of mangoes, this chutney is likely to be rather too expensive to make. But I give it in case some do come your way.*

2 lb (900 g) firm mangoes
12 oz (350 g) onions, finely chopped
1½ lb (675 g) cooking apples peeled, cored and chopped
2 level teaspoons ground ginger

1 pint (600 ml) malt vinegar
3 rounded teaspoons mixed pickling spice
1 lb (450 g) dark soft brown sugar

Peel the mangoes, scraping away any flesh which adheres to it. Cut the flesh away from the stones and cut it into ½ inch (1.25 cm) pieces. Put these into a large saucepan or preserving pan, together with the onions, apples, ginger, and vinegar.

Tie the pickling spice in a piece of muslin and add this to the pan.

Bring the chutney to the boil and then let it simmer for about 40 minutes, stirring frequently, until the ingredients are soft.

Remove the bag of pickling spice from the pan, squeezing it to remove any excess moisture, and then stir in the sugar. Cook the chutney over a low heat, without simmering, until the sugar has dissolved. Then bring to boiling point and allow to simmer for a further 30 minutes, stirring frequently, until it is a fairly thick chutney-like consistency.

Pour into clean hot jars, and cover with vinegar-proof lids to seal.

# Medlar

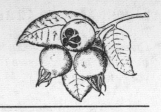

Medlars, either round or pear-shaped, are usually russet coloured with a fringe of thin leaf-like segments round the outside that makes them look rather like rose hips. The skin is tough with a pinkish-brown soft flesh when ripe. They are not widely available in the shops. Their season is late autumn.

The fruit can be eaten as dessert, although it is rather sharp tasting. The medlar's main use is in preserves.

## Medlar Jelly

*This jelly goes very well with venison and with game birds. It is quite simple to make.*

3 lb (1.4 kg) ripe medlars
approximately 1½ pint (900 ml) water

1 lemon
granulated or preserving sugar

Cut up the medlars and put them in a large saucepan. Add just sufficient water to cover and to every 3 lb (1.4 kg) medlars add a whole lemon cut up. Simmer very slowly until the fruit is quite soft and mushy.

Strain through a jelly bag, do not squeeze, and leave to drip overnight.

To every pint (600 ml) juice add 12 oz (350 g) granulated or preserving sugar. Put the juice and sugar into a saucepan and heat slowly until all the sugar has dissolved, then boil rapidly for about 10 minutes until setting point is reached – when a few drops put on a cold saucer form a skin.

Remove from the heat. If necessary skim and then pot and seal in the usual way.

# Melon

Melons come in a wide range of types, and these types can be subdivided into other types, and so on. What they all have in common is their juicy flesh and their large number of seeds. While most melons that we buy are imported, they can be grown successfully in this country, preferably in a greenhouse. They are available in one form or another throughout the year and are served usually as a first course, or added to fruit salad or other mixed fruit sweets.

Different kinds of melon have their own subtle fragrances. Serve with a sprinkling of sugar to bring out the flavour – and then add a sprinkling of ginger to bring out the flavour still more. As a special first course melon is sometimes served with paper-thin Parma ham.

Popular varieties are:

**Cantaloupe**, slightly squat shape, with greenish to yellow, rough segmented skin and pinkish-yellow, heavily scented, flesh.

**Charentais** is small (one serves two people at most), round, with a greenish segmented skin, scented orange flesh, and very sweet.

**Galia** is a small and round, with pale green flesh and rough skin that turns from green to pale-yellow when ripe.

**Honeydew** is the most widely available of all. It is shaped like a rugby ball, has either dark green or pale yellow skin and greenish-yellow, very sweet, flesh. An attractive way to serve a honeydew melon is to cut it in half, remove the seeds and fill the holes with raspberries in jelly, then cut the halves into wedges and the jelly should stay 'set' on the wedge.

**Ogen** is much sought after – and expensive. It has yellow to orange skin marked with faint green stripes. The pale yellow flesh is very sweet and juicy. Serve half or one melon per person.

**Watermelon** is the odd one out. It is by far the largest of the melons and is consequently often sold in slices. The skin is dark green and glossy, the flesh bright red and very juicy, almost watery. Unlike the other types, it has no hollow in the centre and the black seeds are embedded in the flesh. It is available from May to September.

When buying melons, check for ripeness by gently pressing the area round the stalk – it should give slightly – and by smelling the fruit – it should have a sweet fragrance. Store in a cool, dry place.

Melon cut into cubes, slices or balls, can be frozen in syrup for up to one year. Ideally do not thaw completely as it will then be firmer to eat.

**Recipes:**
Melon and Peach Salad, 112
Melon and Prawns à l'Indienne, 113
Minted Chicken and Melon Salad, 113

**Other recipes using melon:**
Green Fruit Salad, 27
Kiwi Fruit, Grape and Melon Salad, 94
Loganberry and Melon Salad, 106
Melon Ice Cream, 191

# Melon and Peach Salad

Serves 4

*If you omit the ham you have an excellent slimmer's lunch, that gives both colour and variety of taste.*

a few lettuce leaves
8 peaches
lemon juice
8 oz (225 g) cottage cheese
4 slices ham, rolled up like a cigar
½ small cantaloupe melon, seeded, peeled and cut into 4 wedges
sprigs of watercress

**Dressing:**
juice of 1 orange
2 level teaspoons caster sugar
1 tablespoon oil
1 tablespoon white wine vinegar
½ level teaspoon Dijon mustard

Arrange a bed of lettuce leaves on a flat serving dish. Skin the peaches by putting them in boiling water for a few minutes until the skin easily peels off. Then halve, remove the stone, brush with lemon juice to prevent discolouration and pile the cottage cheese in the centre of each.

Arrange the stuffed peach halves on the lettuce, putting a slice of rolled ham and a wedge of melon between each peach and pile the watercress in the centre of the dish.

Blend all the dressing ingredients together and serve in a small jug with the salad.

# Melon and Prawns à l'Indienne

Serves 4

*It is essential to add the melon to the flavoured mayonnaise at the last moment, otherwise the prawn mayonnaise sauce will be too runny.*

1 small honeydew melon
¼ pint (150 ml) good quality
   mayonnaise
½ level teaspoon mild curry
   powder

8 oz (225 g) peeled prawns
a little lemon juice
salt
ground black pepper

Cut the top off the melon. Scoop out the seeds and discard them. Cut out the flesh and dice it. Place the pieces in a bowl, cover with foil and chill.

Blend the mayonnaise with the curry powder and stir in the prawns. Add lemon juice and seasoning to taste, cover with foil and chill.

When required take the melon from the refrigerator, drain off any juice and stir the melon into the prawn mayonnaise and mix well. Pile into the empty shell and serve.

# Minted Chicken and Melon Salad

Serves 3 to 4

*This is a deliciously refreshing salad, which could also be made using half a honeydew melon.*

half a galia melon
8 oz (225 g) cold cooked
   chicken
about 3 tablespoons
   mayonnaise

1 tablespoon chopped mint
salt and pepper
a little paprika pepper
lettuce, tomato and mint

Discard the pips from the melon. Remove the flesh with a teaspoon or melon scoop and put in a bowl.

Cut the chicken into neat bite-sized pieces and add to the melon with mayonnaise, chopped mint, salt, pepper and paprika. Mix thoroughly and then taste and check seasoning.

Arrange a bed of lettuce on a dish and spoon the salad on top. Garnish with tomato wedges and a sprig of mint.

# Mulberry

Rather like a blackberry, but larger, the mulberry has a red flesh that deepens to dark-purple when ripe. They are not produced commercially on a large scale and are becoming increasingly scarce. Mulberry trees can sometimes be found in old-fashioned gardens, where, in August, the ripe squashy fruit makes purple stains on the ground beneath. Mulberry leaves were once used to feed silkworms.

The ripe fruit makes a colourful addition to fresh fruit salads. When cooking, it is best to use slightly under-ripe fruit. Freeze in containers and seal.

Recipes:
Mulberry Jelly, 114
Mulberry Layer Cake, 115

See also:
Passion Fruit Profiteroles, 129

Recipe also using mulberries:
Mulberry Ice Cream 191

## Mulberry Jelly

*This jelly is good as a glaze for fruit flans and to serve at teatime. You can expect it to be slightly less set than other jellies.*

6 lb (2.7 kg) mulberries, not
   too ripe

juice of 2 lemons
granulated sugar

Simmer the mulberries with the lemon juice for about 2 hours or until the juice is drawn out and the fruit pulpy. Strain through a jelly bag overnight.

To each pint of juice add 12 oz (350 g) sugar. Put the juice and the sugar in a saucepan, heat gently until the sugar has dissolved, bring to the boil and allow to boil rapidly until setting point is reached. (See Crab Apple Jelly, page 61.)

Pot and seal as usual.

# Mulberry Layer Cake

Serves 8

*This is also very good with fresh raspberries or a mixture of raspberries and peaches.*

6½ oz (187.5 g) butter
6½ oz (187.5 g) castor sugar
8½ oz (237.5 g) flour
2 level teaspoons ground
   cinnamon

½ pint (300 ml) double cream
3 tablespoons top of the milk
12 oz (350 g) mulberries
a little vanilla sugar
icing sugar

Heat the oven to 400°F, 200°C, gas mark 6 and thoroughly grease plenty of baking sheets.

Cream the butter until it is soft, then add the sugar and continue to beat until the mixture is pale and fluffy. Sift the flour and cinnamon together and add to the butter mixture, a tablespoonful at a time. The last few spoonfuls may have to be worked in by hand. Knead lightly and then divide the mixture into 8 equal pieces.

Put one piece of the dough on to the tray and press out very thinly with the fingers to form a 7 inch (17.5 cm) circle. It is a good idea to do this inside a plain flan ring as it gives a nice even circle. Bake in the oven for about 8 minutes until it is a pale golden brown. Remove from the oven and leave to cool for a few minutes before transferring to a wire rack. Repeat with the other 7 pieces of dough, baking two or three at a time, depending on the number of trays that you have.

Whisk the cream and milk together until they form a soft peak. Put the mulberries in a bowl and mash them, with a little vanilla sugar to taste.

Sandwich the layers together with the whipped cream and mashed mulberries, leaving a small amount of cream over for decoration. Leave to stand for 4 hours to allow the mixture to soften slightly before serving.

Put on a serving dish, sprinkle the top with icing sugar and pipe 8 swirls of cream around the edge.

# Nectarine

Nectarines are a variety of peach, but with a smooth skin. The sweet juicy flesh tastes very much the same and the fruit can be used in any recipe that calls for peaches. However, nectarines are nicest eaten raw as a dessert fruit. The season is July to August (home-grown) and December to May and August to September (imported).

Buy fruit that gives gently when placed on the palm of the hand and squeezed (if the greengrocer will let you). It should be evenly shaped and have no blemishes.

To freeze, wipe over the fruit, then halve and remove stones. Slice, sprinkle with lemon juice and pack into containers with a light syrup. Eat the moment the fruit has defrosted or the flesh will discolour.

Recipe:
Nectarine Alaska, 116

For other recipes using nectarines, see Peach

## Nectarine Alaska

Serves 6

*This dish is always very popular with children.*

7 inch (17.5 cm) sponge flan
  case
3 to 4 nectarines

2 egg whites
4 oz (100 g) caster sugar
scoops of vanilla ice cream

Heat the oven to 425 °F, 220 °C, gas mark 7.

Place the sponge flan case on an ovenproof or foil dish. Halve, stone and slice the nectarines and arrange them over the base of the flan case.

Whisk the egg whites until they are stiff and then whisk in the sugar, a spoonful at a time.

Place scoops of ice cream on top of the nectarines. Spread the meringue all over the ice cream so that it is completely sealed.

Bake at once for 5 minutes until the meringue is tinged golden brown. The ice cream will still be firm in the centre.

# Orange

Lemons and limes are bitter; the tangerine family is for Christmas; grapefruit is formal – you have to prepare it with a knife and eat it with a spoon; but the orange is for everybody, at any time. Simply peel it and eat it in your fingers. Dress it up. Make an orange soufflé or a sauce for a roast duck. Drink the juice iced from the refrigerator, enjoy its flavour in a liqueur. The orange is at home anywhere.

This king of citrus fruits can be bought, in one or other of its many varieties, at any time of the year, imported from Brazil, Cyprus, Israel, Italy, Morocco, Spain, Tunisia, from California and Florida. Perhaps the most popular of all, the Jaffa, comes from Israel, large, sweet and juicy, with few pips and a thick skin. Smaller, thinner-skinned varieties are Navels from California and Israel, Valencias from Spain. The blood orange, from Mediterranean countries, has a roughish, reddish skin and red flecks in the flesh; it is very sweet.

These are some of the sweet oranges. There is a bitter variety, the Seville, from Spain. This is used in marmalade and has a short season in January and February.

When buying, go for fruit that feels heavy. Avoid any that are shrivelled or soft.

Choose large juicy oranges to eat for dessert. Use them in fruit salad too. Some of the smaller ones with thinner skins may be better for cooking purposes. When removing the rind, to flavour cakes, puddings, mousses and jellies, for example, use a potato peeler. This enables you to peel the tangy rind thinly from the bitter pith.

To freeze oranges, peel, remove pips and pith and divide into segments. These can be frozen with or without sugar and will keep for about three months without going bitter. When there is a glut of Seville oranges and you do not have time to make your marmalade at once, freeze them whole and store in the freezer until you are ready. Take them from the freezer and make the marmalade by the whole fruit method without thawing them beforehand.

Recipes:

# Pork with Orange and Peppers                    Serves 4

*Use shoulder of pork for this recipe as it has very little fat, yet is not too expensive.*

1¼ lb (550 g) lean pork trimmed of fat and cubed into ½ inch (1.25 cm) pieces
1 large onion, chopped
1 large green pepper, seeded and chopped

2 oranges
1 clove garlic, crushed
salt
freshly ground black pepper
2 level teaspoons made mustard

Fry any trimmings of fat gently in a saucepan to let the fat run out. Lift the pieces of fat pork from the pan and discard, leaving about a tablespoon of fat in the pan. Add the diced pork and onion to the pan and fry quickly for 5 minutes to a pale golden brown. Add the pepper and the grated rind and juice of 1 orange, garlic, seasoning and mustard. Stir until well mixed and then lower the heat. Cover the pan with a tight-fitting lid and simmer gently for about 45 minutes or until the pork is tender.

While the pork is cooking, cut the rind from the remaining orange (see Orange Salad, below) and then cut across in thin slices and cut each slice in quarters. Stir into the pork just before serving. Taste and check seasoning.

Serve with noodles tossed in melted butter.

# Orange Glazed Lamb

Serves 8

*For a change, try this recipe with chicken.*

1 boned shoulder of lamb

*Stuffing:*
1 oz (25 g) butter
1 onion, chopped
3 oz (75 g) fresh white
  breadcrumbs
2 oz (50 g) raisins
1 to 2 level tablespoons
  chopped fresh herbs
grated rind of 1 orange
1 egg, beaten
salt and pepper

*Glaze:*
2 oz (50 g) light soft brown
  sugar
juice of half a lemon
juice of 1 orange
2 tablespoons Worcestershire
  sauce

*Gravy:*
1½ oz (40 g) flour
1 pint (600 ml) stock

Heat the oven to 350 °F, 180 °C, gas mark 4.

Spread out the boned lamb. Make the stuffing: melt the butter in a small saucepan, add the onion and cook gently for 5 minutes or until it is soft. Stir in all the stuffing ingredients and mix well. Spread these over the lamb and press back into shape. Secure with small skewers if necessary. Lay in a meat roasting tin.

Place the glaze ingredients in a pan and cook for 1 minute and then pour them over the lamb. Roast the meat in the oven, basting occasionally, for 2 hours or until the meat is tender. Lift the joint out and put it on a serving dish and keep it warm.

Stir the flour into the pan and cook over a moderate heat for 1 minute. Blend in the stock, stirring continuously until the sauce has thickened. Then simmer for 2 to 3 minutes, taste and check seasoning and serve with the lamb.

# Orange Beef Carbonnade

Serves 6

*Orange combines surprisingly well with most meats. This recipe is also very good if you use pie or stewing veal instead of beef. Serve with buttered noodles or boiled potatoes. A carbonnade makes an excellent dish for entertaining as it can be prepared well in advance and needs little last-minute attention.*

2 lb (900 g) chuck steak
1½ oz (40 g) seasoned flour
2 oz (50 g) dripping
1 large onion, finely sliced
2 cloves garlic, crushed
8 oz (225 g) carrots, finely
    sliced

2 to 3 sticks celery, sliced
½ level teaspoon nutmeg
salt and ground black pepper
¾ pint (450 ml) light ale
grated rind and juice of 1 large
    orange
a little chopped parsley

Heat the oven to 250 °F, 130 °C, gas mark ½.

Cut the meat into 1 inch (2.5 cm) cubes and coat these in the seasoned flour. Melt the dripping in a frying pan and fry the onion and meat to seal. Lift the pieces out with a slotted spoon when they are brown and put them in a casserole. Fry the meat in three or four batches as that way it is much easier to handle and ensures that the meat gets properly sealed.

Add the garlic, carrots and celery to the casserole, together with the nutmeg, seasoning and light ale. Bring to the boil. Cover the casserole and put it into the oven and leave it to cook undisturbed for 4 hours. Then stir in the orange rind and juice and return to the oven for a further hour or until the beef is tender.

Taste and check seasoning. Serve sprinkled with chopped parsley.

# Orange Salad

Serves 6

*This is good with roast venison, duck or goose.*

3 oranges
1 lettuce
small sprigs of watercress

**Dressing:**
6 tablespoons oil
3 tablespoons vinegar
½ level teaspoon salt
plenty of ground black pepper
1 level teaspoon caster sugar

Slice both ends from the oranges, then, standing the fruit upright on a plate, slice down and around the oranges to remove all the peel and pith. Slice each orange across, removing any pips.

Wash and dry the lettuce and watercress and then arrange on a serving dish with the orange slices.

Place all the dressing ingredients together in a small bowl and mix to blend thoroughly. Pour over the orange salad just before serving.

# Crêpes Suzette Makes 10 pancakes

*If you are lucky enough to have a fondue set, this is the kind of recipe you can make at the table. Make the pancakes in advance, have all the ingredients for the sauce ready and prepare it before the very eyes of your guests.*

**Pancakes:**
4 oz (100 g) plain flour
pinch of salt
1 egg
1 tablespoon oil
½ pint (300 ml) milk
oil for frying

**Sauce:**
juice of 2 oranges
4 oz (100 g) unsalted butter
2 oz (50 g) caster sugar
1 tablespoon orange liqueur
3 tablespoons brandy

To make the pancakes: sift the flour and salt into a bowl. Blend the egg, oil and milk together and beat it into the flour to make a fairly thin batter. Heat a very little oil in a 7 inch (17.5 cm) frying pan, add about 2 tablespoons batter to the centre of the pan and tilt and rotate to spread out the batter. Cook for 1 minute, then turn over and cook on the other side for a further minute. Turn out and make 9 more pancakes in the same way.

For the sauce: put the orange juice, butter and sugar in a large frying pan and heat gently until the sugar has dissolved, then simmer gently for 5 minutes, until the sauce is syrupy. Lay one pancake in the pan and coat with the sauce, fold into four and move to one side. Repeat with the rest of the pancakes.

Add the liqueur and brandy to the syrup-covered pancakes, making sure that the pancakes are piping hot. Light with a match. Arrange on a very hot dish and serve at once.

# Caramel Oranges

Serves 6

*Serve these really cold. The same recipe can be made using slices or wedges, rather than whole oranges.*

| | |
|---|---|
| 6 oranges | 2 tablespoons brandy |
| 4 oz (100 g) granulated sugar | 5 tablespoons water |

Thinly peel the rind from two oranges with a potato peeler and cut it into very thin julienne strips. Place these in a small saucepan, cover with cold water, bring to the boil and simmer for 20 minutes or until tender. Drain and reserve.

Slice both ends from the oranges and stand them upright on a plate. Slice down and around the oranges to remove all the peel and pith. Slice each orange across, removing any pips, and then put it back into its original shape and secure it with wooden cocktail sticks. Arrange in a dish.

Reserve all the orange juice on the plate and put it into a measure with the brandy and make up to ¼ pint (150 ml) with water.

Place the sugar and 5 tablespoons of cold water in a small thick pan and stir over a low heat until the sugar has dissolved, then bring to the boil and cook rapidly to a rich dark caramel. Remove from the heat and stir in the orange juice mixture – be careful as it will splutter. Return the pan to the heat and warm it until the caramel and orange juice have amalgamated to form a sauce. Pour over the oranges, leave to cool and then chill thoroughly overnight.

Next day put the oranges in a serving dish, spoon over the syrup, sprinkle with the strips of orange and serve with a bowl of whipped cream.

# Orange Sherbert

Serves 6

*A Lemon Sherbert can be made by following this recipe, but you would need to use 6 lemons.*

| | |
|---|---|
| 4 oranges | 6 oz (175 g) sugar |
| ½ pint (300 ml) water | 3 egg whites |

Peel the rind thinly from 2 oranges and put in a saucepan with the water and sugar. Heat gently until the sugar has dissolved, then simmer for 10 minutes. Remove the saucepan from the heat and leave to cool.

Cut the oranges in half and scoop out all the flesh, together with the juice, into a bowl. Remove the pips and then sieve the flesh or purée it in a blender. Strain the sugar syrup on to the orange purée and mix well. Turn the mixture into a rigid container, cover and freeze until half frozen.

Whisk the egg whites until they are stiff. Turn the half-frozen orange mixture into a bowl and whisk it until it is smooth. Fold in the egg whites and then return to the container and cover. Freeze until firm, and label.

When required, transfer the sherbert to the refrigerator for about 15 minutes to soften it slightly, then spoon into glasses and serve.

# Orange Cider Sauce                                     Serves 4

*This is a piquant sauce and good to serve with grilled meat. Add any juices in the grill pan to the sauce to add extra flavour.*

1 oz (25 g) butter
1 small onion, chopped
grated rind and juice of 1
 orange
1 clove garlic, crushed
1 level tablespoon tomato
 purée

½ level teaspoon Dijon mustard
¼ pint (150 ml) chicken stock
½ pint (300 ml) cider
salt and pepper
1 level tablespoon caster sugar
2 level tablespoons cornflour
2 tablespoons water

Melt the butter in a small saucepan and add the onion, orange rind and garlic and fry gently for 5 minutes. Add the tomato purée, mustard, chicken stock, cider, seasoning, sugar and orange juice. Bring to the boil, stirring frequently, and then reduce the heat and simmer for 30 minutes or longer if possible. A long slow cook for a sauce like this greatly improves the flavour.

In a cup or small bowl blend the cornflour with the water to a smooth paste and stir it into the sauce. Bring to the boil, stirring constantly until thickened. Simmer for 3 to 4 minutes and taste and check seasoning.

Serve with grilled pork or gammon.

# Orange and Lemon Sugars

*Keep fruit-flavoured sugars in jars in the larder and use when making cakes, biscuits and puddings.*

Grate orange or lemon rind on the finest grater and mix it with caster sugar. Allow 4 oz (100 g) caster sugar to each fruit used.

Put the sugar and zest together in a bowl and work them together with a wooden spoon until the sugar has taken the colour from the zest and absorbed all the oil from the rind.

Spread the sugar out on a piece of greaseproof paper or foil and allow it to dry. If lumpy, sieve it and then store in a clean airtight jar.

# Seville Orange and Apricot Marmalade   Makes about 7 to 8 lb (3.2 to 3.6 kg)

*This really is very good and a great favourite with people who do not like a very sharp marmalade.*

2 lb (900 g) Seville oranges
1 lemon
6 oz (175 g) dried apricots

4 pints (2.3 litres) water
5 lb (2.3 kg) granulated sugar

Wash the oranges and lemon, cut them in half, squeeze out the juice into a large bowl and scrape the pith from the fruit with a teaspoon and put it, with the pips, in a smaller bowl.

Shred the orange and lemon skins finely and cut the dried apricots in quarters and put them in the large bowl with the juice. Add 3 pints (1.7 litres) water and put the other pint (600 ml) over the pips and pith. Leave both containers for at least 24 hours to soak. This process softens the peel and swells the apricots.

Put the pith and pips in a piece of muslin and tie with string to form a bag. Add any remaining water from the pips to the pan of fruit and water. Bring to the boil and simmer without a lid for 30 minutes or until the fruit is tender. Remove the muslin bag, add the sugar to the pan and stir until it has dissolved, then boil rapidly until setting point is reached. (See Crab Apple Jelly, page 61.) Skim, remove from the heat and leave to cool.

Pot in warm jars, cover and label.

# Dark Mature Marmalade

Makes about 10 lb (4.5 kg)

*Muscovado is a very dark and natural sugar and adds a lovely flavour to the marmalade.*

3 lb (1.4 kg) Seville oranges
5 pints (2.8 litres) water
juice of 2 lemons

5½ lb (2.5 kg) granulated sugar
8 oz (225 g) muscovado sugar

Wash the oranges and place them in a large saucepan with 4 pints (2.3 litres) of water. Simmer gently without a lid for about 2 hours or until the fruit is quite soft. Test with a sharp knife.

With a perforated spoon, lift out the oranges, keeping the water they have been cooked in.

When cold enough to handle, halve the fruit and scoop out the pulp, pips and pith into a clean saucepan. Add the remaining pint (600 ml) water and cook gently for about 20 minutes to extract the pectin. Strain and discard the pulp and pips.

Cut up coarsely the softened orange peel and add to the liquid in the first saucepan. Add the strained water from the pan containing the pulp and pips. Add the lemon juice and both sugars. Stir over a low heat until the sugars have dissolved. Bring to the boil and boil rapidly for approximately 15 to 20 minutes until setting point is reached. (See Crab Apple Jelly, page 61.) Draw the pan from the heat and skim.

Leave to cook, then stir and pot in clean warm jars, cover and label.

# Fresh Fruit Squash

*If you like a sharper tasting squash, use 2 large lemons instead of the orange and lemon*

| | |
|---|---|
| 1 orange | 1¼ to 1½ lb (550 to 675 g) |
| 1 lemon | granulated sugar |
| 2 pints (a good litre) water | 1 oz (25 g) citric acid |

Use a potato peeler to cut away, very thinly, the orange and lemon peel. Cut the fruit in half and squeeze out the juice.

Place the peel in a blender with some of the measured water and switch on to top speed for 30 seconds, then pour into a saucepan with remaining water and bring to the boil.

Add the sugar, fruit juice and citric acid, lower the heat and stir until the sugar has dissolved.

Strain and pour into hot sterilised bottles. Screw the caps in place, cool and then use as required, diluting with water or soda.

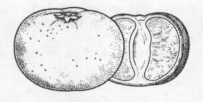

# Ortanique

An ortanique is a cross between an orange and a tangerine. It has orange-yellow thin skin and sweet, juicy, orange-coloured flesh. Supplies are imported from Spain and the West Indies.

Use it as a dessert fruit or in marmalade. To prepare ortanqiue sections, peel sufficiently thickly as to remove all white pith, starting at one end and removing the peel in one continuous strip if you can. Hold the fruit over a bowl to collect any juice. Loosen each segment and remove from the surrounding membrane.

Recipe:
Ortanique Bristol, 127

For other recipes using
ortaniques, see Orange

# Ortanique Bristol

Serves 4

*Serve very cold with whisked thick custard blended with an equal quantity of whipped cream. If you like you can use oranges instead of ortaniques, and pears may be substituted for the apples.*

6 oz (175 g) granulated sugar
¾ pint (450 ml) water
5 Cox's eating apples
2 ortaniques

*Caramel:*
3 oz (75 g) granulated sugar
¼ pint (150 ml) water

First make the caramel: dissolve the sugar in the water, then boil rapidly, without stirring, until a golden brown. Remove from the heat and pour over an oiled enamel plate and leave to set. Crush into small pieces.

Put the sugar and water into a saucepan. Dissolve the sugar over a gentle heat, then boil rapidly for 1 minute. Peel, quarter and core the apples and cut each quarter in three and poach gently for 10 minutes. Remove from the heat and leave to cool.

Remove the rind from 1 ortanique with a potato peeler and cut into very thin shreds. Place these in a small saucepan, cover with water and simmer for 5 minutes, drain and rinse.

Remove the skin and pith from both ortaniques (see Orange Salad, page 120) and then divide the flesh into neat segments. Add this to the apples, stir lightly to mix and then turn into a glass serving dish. Sprinkle over the orange shreds. Just before serving scatter over the crushed caramel.

# Passion Fruit

Glamorous and exciting as this tropical fruit may sound, it is not much to look at – rather like a large wrinkled plum. The tough skin is purple, the flesh orange-coloured, sweet and juicy and full of black seeds which are eaten along with the flesh. The fruit is available sporadically throughout the year but is not easily tracked down in local shops. More commonly it can be bought, in cans and used in fruit salads, jellies and sorbets.

Eat it fresh when you can get hold of it. The fruit should be halved and the stone removed, the flesh then scooped out with a small spoon and eaten with sugar. Use the tangy juice to flavour cocktails, punches and fruit cups.

Passion fruit stores well in the refrigerator but should be removed and used before the skins become too wrinkled.

**Recipe:**
Passion Fruit Sorbet, 128      Passion Fruit Profiteroles, 129


## Passion Fruit Sorbet          Serves 4

*This is a very simple, but rather special, dessert.*

2 passion fruit                sherry

Halve the passion fruit, remove the stones and scoop out the flesh. With a fork, mash the flesh to a pulp.

Mix the passion fruit pulp with sherry in the proportion two-thirds passion fruit to one-third sherry. Spoon the mixture into 4 individual wine glasses, chill and serve.

# Passion Fruit Profiteroles

Serves 6 to 8

*Profiteroles make a marvellous dessert for a dinner party. Instead of filling them with passion fruit, you can use halved black cherries, mulberries or sliced kiwi fruit.*

2 oz (50 g) butter
¼ pint (150 ml) water
2½ oz (62 g) plain flour
2 eggs, beaten

**Filling:**
½ pint (300 ml) double cream
3 to 4 passion fruit
sugar to taste

**Icing:**
1½ oz (40 g) butter
1 oz (25 g) cocoa
4 oz (100 g) icing sugar
3 to 4 tablespoons evaporated milk

Heat the oven to 425 °F, 220 °C, gas mark 7. Grease a baking tray.

Put the butter and water in a small pan and bring to the boil slowly to allow the butter to melt. Remove from the heat and add the flour all at once and beat until it forms a ball. Gradually beat in the eggs a little at a time to make a smooth shiny paste.

Put the mixture into a piping bag fitted with a ½ inch (1.25 cm) plain nozzle and pipe into 20 blobs on the baking tray and bake for 10 minutes. Then reduce the heat to 375 °F, 190 °C, gas mark 5 for a further 15 to 20 minutes until the balls are well risen and golden brown. Split one side of each bun to allow the steam to escape and leave to cool on a wire rack.

Lightly whip the cream until it will hold a gentle peak, scoop the flesh out of the passion fruit and stir into the cream with sugar to taste. Use this mixture to fill the buns.

Now make the icing: melt the butter in a small pan and stir in the cocoa and cook gently for 1 minute. Remove the pan from the heat and stir in the sieved icing sugar and evaporated milk. Beat well until it starts to thicken.

Spear each bun with a fork and dip into the icing to just cover the tops. Pile up the profiteroles in a pyramid on a serving dish as each one is finished.

Serve on the day they are made.

# Peach

The peach used to be one of the great English fruits. Provided you had a sunny wall or, better still, a hothouse and the money to support it all, you could produce fruit that could hardly have an equal in the world. Even today, the home-produced peach, with its slightly greenish tinge, has an incomparable flavour. The trouble is that it cannot be produced in quantity.

There is a big market for peaches; and there is a good number of countries that can supply them in quantity, and of excellent quality too. We now import peaches from South Africa (January to March), France (June to August), Italy (June to September). The season for home-grown fruit is June to August.

There are two types of peach, freestone and clingstone. The main difference is that in the latter the stone is more difficult to remove from the flesh. The skin may be pale-yellow to orange, tinged with pink, and with a soft bloom on it – the proverbial peach-like complexion. English hothouse peaches often have a faint greenish tinge. The flesh is usually orangey-yellow, very sweet and juicy.

When buying, avoid split or bruised fruit. Choose those that give to a gentle squeeze in the palm of the hand.

Eat ripe peaches as dessert. Use them in innumerable dishes – Peach Melba is the first that comes to mind. There are peach tarts, flans, mousses; fruit salads benefit from the addition of a few skinned and quartered peaches. (To remove the skin, put the fruit in boiling water briefly, then in cold and the skin will peel off.) They can also be made into jam.

Peaches can be frozen, whole, halved or sliced in syrup. Serve as soon as they have thawed, or the flesh will discolour. They are also, of course, available, and very popular, canned.

## Sweet and Sour Gammon

Serves 4

*You can serve pineapple slices with the gammon instead of peaches if you like.*

4 gammon or bacon steaks
butter
2 fresh peaches
1½ level tablespoons cornflour
½ pint (300 ml) water

1 tablespoon soy sauce
2 tablespoons vinegar
2 level tablespoons demerara
  sugar

Heat the oven to 375 °F, 190 °C, gas mark 5.

Place the gammon steaks in a shallow ovenproof dish; if they are very fatty trim off any excess fat. Dot with a little butter.

Skin the peaches, cut them in half and remove the stones and lay a half on top of each piece of gammon. Cover with foil and bake in the oven for about 20 minutes, by which time the peach and gammon will both be tender.

Meanwhile, put the cornflour in a saucepan and stir in the water, soy sauce, vinegar and demerara sugar. Bring slowly to the boil, stirring until the mixture has thickened and then simmer for 5 minutes. Taste and, if necessary, add a little salt and pepper.

Remove the gammon from the oven, lift out on to a serving dish and spoon the sauce over.

# Fruit Brûlée

Serves 8

*There is no need to serve cream with a brûlée as the topping is a thickened cream in itself. Serve small portions as it is very rich.*

4 peaches, pears or 8 apricots
8 oz (225 g) caster sugar or
 vanilla sugar
1 pint (600 ml) water

*Brûlée:*
5 egg yolks
1 oz (25 g) vanilla sugar or
 caster sugar and vanilla
 essence
1 pint (600 ml) single cream
about 2 oz (50 g) demerara
 sugar

Peel, halve and stone the peaches, pears or apricots.

Put the caster sugar and water in a large shallow pan and simmer together, stirring occasionally, until the sugar has dissolved. Add the fruit and poach gently for about 10 minutes, then lift out with a slotted spoon and drain thoroughly on kitchen paper.

Heat the oven to 325 °F, 160 °C, gas mark 3. Well butter a shallow ovenproof dish, about 2 pint (1.1 litre) size. Arrange the fruit in it.

Beat the egg yolks with the vanilla or caster sugar: if you do not have vanilla sugar, add a little vanilla essence. Heat the cream to scalding (180 °F, 82 °C) and gradually beat it into the egg yolks. Pour the mixture into the dish and stand in a baking tin half filled with warm water and bake in the oven for 45 minutes or until set. Take out and leave to cool.

Sprinkle the top of the brûlée with demerara sugar to about ¼ inch (6 mm) thickness and put the dish under a hot grill. Watch carefully until the sugar melts and caramelises to a golden brown. Remove and chill for about 3 hours before serving. This gives time for the hard caramel topping to become less hard and easy to crack and serve.

Do not leave it longer before serving as the caramel will melt and soften, spoiling the appearance and the taste of the brûlée.

# Quick Fruit Brûlée

For a quick fruit brûlée, put a thick layer of peaches or some other fruit that does not need cooking, such as raspberries, strawberries or grapes, in a heat-proof dish, then cover with whipped cream blended with an equal quantity of plain yogurt. Chill in the refrigerator for an hour or two, then sprinkle with demerara sugar and brown under a hot grill. Delicious!

## Sparkling Peaches                                        Serves 6

*It is essential to serve this dessert very cold. It is deliciously refreshing after a big meal.*

4 oz (100 g) granulated sugar       ½ pint (300 ml) sweet cider
¼ pint (150 ml) water              3 tablespoons brandy
6 ripe peaches

Put the sugar in a saucepan with the water and heat gently over a low heat until it has dissolved. Then remove from the heat and cool.

Put the peaches in a basin and cover with boiling water. Leave for a minute, then turn all the peaches at once into a bowl of cold water and remove the skins by gently peeling them off. Prick each peach with a stainless steel fork right through to the stone in several places. As each peach is peeled and pricked put them into a glass bowl just big enough to take 6. Cover with first the sugar syrup and then ¼ pint (150 ml) cider and the brandy so that the peaches are completely immersed. Cover with cling film and chill in the refrigerator for at least 6 hours. At the same time, chill the remaining ¼ pint (150 ml) cider.

Just before serving, remove from the refrigerator and stir the chilled cider into the peaches; this will make the peach juice fizzle and sparkle. Serve with a bowl of lightly whipped thick cream.

# Peach Melba

Serves 4

*This is a real peach melba. Home-made raspberry sauce is so much better than the bottled variety. You can use frozen raspberries for this recipe but make sure that they have been properly thawed first.*

4 fresh peaches
8 oz (225 g) caster sugar
1 pint (600 ml) water

**Raspberry sauce:**
8 oz (225 g) fresh raspberries
  or frozen without sugar
2 tablespoons red currant jelly
2 level teaspoons cornflour
1 tablespoon water
home-made or bought vanilla
  ice cream

Peel, halve and stone the peaches. Put the caster sugar and water in a large shallow pan and simmer together, stirring occasionally, until the sugar has dissolved. Put the peaches in a single layer and simmer gently for about 10 minutes, then remove from the heat and leave to cool in the syrup. When quite cold, lift out the peaches with a slotted spoon.

For the sauce: put the raspberries, with the red currant jelly, in a saucepan and stir over a moderate heat, mashing down until the jelly has melted and the raspberries are quite soft. Blend the cornflour with the water and stir it into the contents of the pan. Bring it to the boil, stirring continuously until the mixture has thickened and become clear. Turn into a bowl and leave to become quite cold.

Place a portion of ice cream in the base of 4 sundae glasses and arrange 2 peach halves on top. Spoon the raspberry sauce over and serve at once.

# Pear

Pears are grown in this country: dessert pears are produced in hothouses or on walls and the normal garden tree provides cooking varieties, usually sour and rather hard. Large quantities of dessert pears are imported and can be bought throughout the year. Like apples, pears divide into dessert and cooking varieties. The skins vary from green to russet, with creamy yellow flesh. There is a core in the centre and a few pips. The perfect dessert pear should be juicy and have a strong but delicious scent.

The most popular dessert pears are Conference, Comice and William. Remember that they are delicate fruit and bruise easily. They are best bought before they are fully ripe and left in the airing cupboard for two or three days. Check for ripeness by pressing gently at the stalk end – the fruit should yield a little.

Eat pears as a dessert, in a trifle or a fruit salad, or cooked as apples. Add ripe ones to salads, bake firm pears in foil with lemon juice, sugar and cinnamon or stew them in wine until tender. Hard pears benefit greatly from long, slow cooking – it brings out their delicate flavour.

They can be frozen uncooked, peeled and quartered and covered with a light syrup, and stored for up to eight months.

# Stilton Pears

Serves 4

*If you have no Stilton to hand, use Danish blue; both make a piquant dressing.*

8 slices cold roast pork
4 ripe Comice pears
lemon juice
a little mustard and cress

*Stilton dressing:*
2 oz (50 g) Stilton cheese,
    crumbled
1 teaspoon Worcestershire
    sauce
1 tablespoon mayonnaise
1 pickled onion, finely chopped
4 tablespoons French dressing
a little salt
freshly ground black pepper

Arrange 4 slices of meat down the long sides of a flat serving dish.
 Peel, core and halve the pears and brush them with a little lemon juice and place them down the centre of the dish.
 Place all the dressing ingredients together in a bowl and mix well; take care not to add too much salt. Spoon the dressing over the pears and garnish with mustard and cress.
 Serve with hot herb bread.

# New England Salad

Serves 4

*This is an unusual salad. It is essential that the spinach is very young and very fresh.*

4 oz (100 g) young spinach
3 tablespoons French dressing
2 dessert pears
salt and pepper
4 oz (100 g) Cheddar cheese,
    grated

2 oz (50 g) button mushrooms,
    sliced
2 tomatoes
2 hard-boiled eggs, sliced
sprig of parsley

Remove the thick centre stalk from the spinach. Wash and drain thoroughly and then shred the leaves finely and toss in 1 tablespoonful of French dressing. Core and slice the pears and coat in another tablespoon of dressing.

Arrange the spinach in the bottom of a salad bowl, then add a layer of pear. Season, then add the cheese in one layer. Toss the mushrooms in the remaining dressing and then spoon on top of the cheese. Arrange the eggs with the rest of the pears over the mushrooms. Decorate with sliced tomato and a sprig of parsley.

# Pear and Ginger Trifle                                    Serves 6

*This trifle can be adapted for use with other fruits.*

8 oz (225 g) cooking pears
6 tablespoons water
3 tablespoons ginger wine
2 oz (50 g) granulated sugar
6 individual sponge cakes, split
  in half
apricot jam
2 pieces stem ginger, chopped

3 egg yolks
1 oz (25 g) caster sugar
1 heaped teaspoon cornflour
½ pint (300 ml) milk
¼ pint (150 ml) whipping cream
½ oz (12.5 g) flaked almonds,
  browned

Peel, core and dice the pears. Place the water, ginger wine and sugar in a saucepan and heat gently until the sugar has dissolved, then add the diced pears and poach them for 3 to 4 minutes until they are soft but still holding their shape.

Sandwich the sponge cakes together with apricot jam. Place them in a 2 pint (a good litre) serving dish. Spoon the pears and the syrup over the top and sprinkle with chopped stem ginger.

Mix together the egg yolks, sugar and cornflour. Warm the milk in a saucepan over a low heat until it is hand-hot, then pour it on to the egg yolk mixture, stirring constantly. Return the mixture to the saucepan and cook gently, stirring constantly, until it thickens. Do not allow the custard to boil or it will curdle. When thickened, leave it to cool, then pour it over the sponge cakes and leave to set.

When the custard has set, lightly whisk the cream until it is thick and then spread it over the custard. Sprinkle with the almonds and serve.

# Pear and Mincemeat Slice                    Serves 8

*An ideal recipe to use when you have a glut of pears (or apples) in the garden; the fruit need not even be ripe. Delicious served warm with ice cream.*

14 oz (397 g) packet puff pastry      2 to 3 pears
half a 1 lb (450 g) jar                      granulated sugar
  mincemeat

Heat the oven to 425 °F, 220 °C, gas mark 7.

Roll out the pastry to a strip 24 by 9 inches (61 by 22.5 cm) and cut across in half. Take one piece of pastry, fold it in half lengthwise and cut 2 inch (5 cm) slits along the folded edge, about ½ inch (1.25 cm) apart. Open it out again.

Place the plain piece of pastry on a baking sheet and spread over the mincemeat leaving a 1 inch (2.5 cm) border around the edge.

Peel, core and slice the pears and arrange these on top of the mincemeat. Damp the edges of the pastry and cover with the cut piece of pastry. Press the edges firmly together to seal.

Brush the surface of the pastry with cold water and sprinkle with granulated sugar. Bake in the oven for 35 to 40 minutes until the pastry has risen and is golden brown and the pears are tender.

Serve warm with ice cream.


# Pears Elizabeth                             Serves 6

*This looks spectacular. Chocolate blends very well with pears.*

3½ oz (100 g) bar plain             2 oz (50 g) shelled walnuts
  chocolate                              2 oz (50 g) glacé cherries
3 eggs separated                     6 dessert pears

Break the chocolate into squares. Place these in a bowl and stand it over a pan of simmering water until the chocolate has melted. Then remove from the heat. Stir in the egg yolks.

Whisk the egg whites until they are stiff and carefully fold them into the chocolate mixture. Leave on one side.

Roughly chop the walnuts and cherries, leaving 3 cherries whole for decoration.

Carefully core each pear, with an apple corer, from the opposite end to the stalk and remove all the pips with a pointed spoon, but do not cut right through the stalk. Cut a slice from the base of each pear so that they will stand upright.

Pack the pears tightly with the walnut and cherry mixture and place in individual serving dishes. Spoon chocolate mousse over each pear and then chill.

Decorate each pear with half a cherry and serve with single cream.

## Spiced Pickled Pears          Makes about 8 lb (3.6 kg)

*These are very good with cold meat. Once opened, keep the jar in the refrigerator.*

4 lb (1.8 kg) granulated sugar
2 pints (a good litre) malt
  vinegar
thinly peeled rind of 1 lemon
½ oz (12.5 g) cloves
½ oz (12.5 g) allspice
¼ oz (6.5 g) root ginger
small piece cinnamon stick
8 lb (3.6 kg) firm pears
salt

Put the sugar in a preserving pan with the vinegar and leave to dissolve over a low heat. Put the lemon rind, cloves, allspice, ginger and cinnamon stick into a piece of muslin, tie it with a string to form a bag and add it to the pan.

Peel, quarter and core pears and drop them into a salt and water solution to prevent them going brown. When they are all prepared, rinse in cold water and add to the pan. Cover and allow the pears to simmer very gently for about 20 to 30 minutes until they are translucent and tender.

When the pears are tender, drain them and arrange neatly in 1 lb (450 g) jars. You will need about 8 of these. Boil the liquid in the pan rapidly for 5 minutes until it is the consistency of thin syrup, then pour it over the pears while it is still hot.

Cover and seal the pears and leave to mature for about 3 months before using.

# Pears in Cider

Serves 4

*Pears have a very delicate flavour which is brought out by cooking them in cider.*

1½ lb (675 g) cooking pears      4 cloves
4 oz (100 g) granulated sugar      ½ pint (300 ml) sweet cider

Peel, quarter and core the pears and place them in a saucepan with the sugar, cloves and cider. Add a few drops of cochineal, cover and simmer gently until the pears are tender; this will take about 30 to 45 minutes.

Remove the cloves and turn the pears into a serving dish. They may then be served either hot or cold with whipped cream.

# Persimmon

Persimmon, kaki or date plum, looks like a large tomato, with a leathery skin and orange pulp. A few varieties are seedless. One type, called sharon fruit, has an edible skin as well as being free of pips. The flesh is sweet and is delicious raw, eaten when it is really ripe. Persimmons are also used in jellies and jams.

All supplies of this fruit in Britain are imported and are available in the shops from October to January.

## Sharon Ring Layer

Serves 8

*This is a different type of gâteau, made with sharon fruit, but you could try using peaches or nectarines for a change.*

*Sponge ring:*
3 eggs, separated
3 oz (75 g) caster sugar
3 oz (75 g) plain flour
1 level teaspoon baking powder

*Custard cream:*
3 egg yolks
3 level tablespoons flour
3 level tablespoons caster sugar
¾ pint (450 ml) milk
½ oz (12.5 g) butter

2 to 4 tablespoons fruit juice or orange liqueur
3 tablespoons apricot jam
1 tablespoon lemon juice
2 sharon fruit
¼ pint (150 ml) double or whipping cream
6 lightly crushed brandy snaps

Heat the oven to 325 °F, 160 °C, gas mark 3. Lightly oil a 2 pint (1.1 litre) ring mould.

Whisk the egg whites with an electric or hand rotary whisk until very stiff. Whisk in the egg yolks one at a time, and then whisk in the sugar, still keeping the mixture stiff.

Sift the flour and baking powder together and fold into the egg whites. Turn the sponge mixture into the prepared ring mould and bake in the oven for 30 minutes, until the sponge is a pale golden brown and has shrunk slightly away from the sides of the tin. Carefully turn out and leave to cool on a wire rack.

Meanwhile, make the custard cream. In a bowl, mix the egg yolks, flour and sugar with a little of the milk to make a smooth paste. Heat the remaining milk and, when hot but not boiling, pour on to the egg yolk mixture and stir until smooth. Rinse out the saucepan and return the custard to the pan. Cook over a gentle heat, stirring until the custard is thick and smooth. (This will take about 3 minutes.) Do not allow the custard to boil. Add the knob of butter and leave to cool, stirring occasionally to prevent a skin forming.

Slice the sponge ring across twice to give 3 equal ring slices. Place the lower sponge ring on a serving plate and sprinkle with half the fruit juice or liqueur. Coat the top and sides with the custard cream and fill in the hollow.

Melt the apricot jam and lemon juice, stirring until blended, and then brush over the sides of the remaining sponge rings.

Place the middle sponge layer on the custard and sprinkle with the remaining fruit juice or liqueur. Slice 1 sharon fruit into 8 or 9 slices and arrange on the sponge ring, cover with the last piece of sponge.

Whisk the cream until it is thick and forms soft peaks and then spread over the top sponge layer. Put any remaining cream in the centre hole.

Pile the brandy snaps in the centre and slice the remaining sharon fruit into 6 slices, cut each slice from the edge to the centre, twist and place on the cream.

# Pineapple

The pineapple is a large, oval, tropical fruit with a hard brownish knobbly skin. A crown of stiff spiky leaves protrudes from the top. Pull out a leaf from the centre of the crown – if it comes out easily the fruit is ripe. The flesh is firm, yellow to cream in colour, juicy and sweet. The fruit is available all the year round.

Pineapples are delicious eaten fresh. Peel thickly to remove all the skin. Take out the hard core and slice or dice the flesh. Alternatively, cut in half lengthwise and scoop the flesh out of the skin, dice it, sugar it, mix it with liqueur if you like, and pile it back into the shell. Or serve it filled with fruit salad or ice cream. One of the nicest and simplest ways to serve a pineapple is to cut it into four or six wedges; keep the green on and cut down or across depending on the size. Cut underneath and serve one wedge per person, like melon, with a twist of orange on top. Use pineapple as a garnish for cakes and sweets, or in salads, diced in puddings, or chopped in tarts.

You can, of course, buy pineapple in canned form, in rings or chunks – try the rings as pineapple fritters. The juice is sold canned or bottled.

To freeze pineaple, remove the rind and slice the flesh, cover with syrup and keep in a rigid container.

# Chicken with Pineapple

Serves 4

*This is a colourful dish – and very good.*

4 chicken portions
1½ oz (40 g) seasoned flour
2 oz (50 g) butter
1 onion, sliced
1 green pepper, seeded and
  sliced
½ pint (300 ml) chicken stock

2 tablespoons light brown
  sugar
2 tablespoons vinegar
4 tablespoons tomato ketchup
salt and pepper
4 slices fresh pineapple

Lightly coat the chicken in the seasoned flour. Melt the butter in a large saucepan and fry the chicken on both sides to brown. Lift out the pieces and put them on one side.

Add the onion and green pepper to the saucepan and fry for 3 minutes, then stir in the remaining flour and cook for a minute. Stir in the stock, sugar, vinegar and tomato ketchup and bring to the boil, stirring until the sauce has thickened. Season well and then return the chicken portions to the saucepan, cover with a tight fitting lid and simmer for 30 minutes.

Remove the peel from the pineapple. Cut out the core in the centre and cut each slice in half. Add these to the saucepan and cook for a further 20 to 30 minutes or until the chicken is tender.

Taste and check seasoning, turn into a warm dish and serve.

# Pineapple and Ham
# Cornet Salad

Serves 4

*Pineapple and ham go extremely well together.*

3 oz (75 g) white cabbage,
  finely shredded
4 pickled onions, thinly sliced
2 gherkins, chopped
4 slices fresh pineapple
3 tablespoons thick mayonnaise

salt
freshly ground black pepper
8 thin slices cooked ham
1 small Webb's lettuce, finely
  shredded

Put the cabbage and pickled onions in a bowl, together with the gherkins and 1 slice of pineapple finely diced. Then stir in the mayonnaise and season well. Lay the slices of ham flat, divide the cabbage mixture between them and roll them up like a cornet.

Pile the lettuce on a serving platter and arrange the cornets of ham on top. Cut 1 slice of pineapple into 8 wedges and place a piece on top of each cornet. Then quarter the remaining 2 slices of pineapple and arrange around the edge of the dish.

# Jellied Salad                                     Serves 4

*You either like this kind of dish or you do not. It is very colourful and American.*

1 lemon jelly
just under ½ pint (300 ml)
   boiling water
3 tablespoons cider vinegar
1 level teaspoon salt
freshly ground black pepper
2 tomatoes, skinned and each
   cut into 6 wedges

2 slices pineapple, each cut into
   12 wedges
1 carrot, grated
1 dill cucumber, sliced
lettuce
mustard and cress

Lightly oil a 1 pint (600 ml) ring mould. Dissolve the jelly in the water, add the vinegar, salt and pepper. Place 12 tomato wedges around the base of the mould and between each tomato place a wedge of pineapple. Pour half the jelly on top and then cover this with grated carrot.

Put the slices of dill cucumber around the inside edge of the mould and the other 12 wedges of pineapple like a flower around the top of the carrot. Pour the rest of the jelly over the top and chill in the refrigerator until set.

Turn out the mould on to a bed of lettuce and fill the centre with mustard and cress.

Serve with a selection of cold cooked meats.

# Fresh Pineapple and Ginger Meringue

Serves 6 to 8

*This is absolutely delicious. The meringue is slightly tacky because it is made with brown sugar. If you want a really firm meringue, use half caster and half soft brown sugar. It can be made equally well with fresh pears.*

4 egg whites
8 oz (225 g) light soft brown
   sugar

*Filling:*
8 oz (225 g) fresh pineapple,
   chopped finely
½ pint (300 ml) whipping
   cream whipped
2 to 3 pieces stem ginger, finely
   chopped

Heat the oven to 200 °F, 100 °C, gas mark ¼.

Line 2 large baking sheets with non-stick silicone paper. On one baking tray mark out a circle 8 inches (20 cm) in diameter. On the other baking tray mark one circle 7 inches (17.5 cm) in diameter and another circle 6 inches (15 cm) in diameter; use plates and saucers as guides.

Place the egg whites in a large bowl and whisk on high speed until they form soft peaks. Add the sugar a teaspoonful at a time, whisking well after each addition, until all the sugar has been added.

Divide the meringue between the marked circles and spread it evenly to cover. Bake in the oven for 3 to 4 hours, until the meringues are firm to touch and dried out. Remove from the oven, leave to cool and then peel off the paper.

Place the pineapple, cream and ginger in a bowl and stir until well blended. Put the largest circle of meringue on a serving plate and spread with half the pineapple filling, then cover with the next size of meringue and spread over the remaining cream filling and place the smallest meringue layer on top. Leave to stand for at least 1 hour before serving.

# Pineapple in Kirsch

Serves 6

*A very simple recipe, but it is essential that you serve it very cold. For real luxury serve it with pineapple ice cream.*

1 pineapple                                    2 tablespoons Kirsch
2 tablespoons caster sugar

Slice off the leaf and stem end of the pineapple and keep the leaves on one side. Cut the pineapple across into ½ inch (1.25 cm) slices and, using a small sharp knife, cut off the skin from each slice.

Remove the tough centre core with a small pastry cutter or an apple corer.

Arrange the slices on a flat serving dish and sprinkle with sugar and Kirsch. Leave covered with foil in a cool place for at least 8 hours so that the fruit is thoroughly chilled.

When ready to serve, arrange the leaves, standing them upright, in the centre of the dish.

Serve with a bowl of softly whipped cream.

# Pineapple Flambé

Serves 6

*Another very simple pineapple recipe. Make it the moment you need it. You can, if you like, use bananas instead of pineapple.*

1 pineapple                                    2 oz (50 g) light soft brown sugar
2 oz (50 g) unsalted butter          3 tablespoons brandy

Prepare the pineapple in slices as in Pineapple in Kirsch (above). Melt the butter in a frying pan and fry the pineapple in the hot butter until it just begins to colour. Sprinkle over the sugar, add the brandy and set alight.

Let the flames burn for a few seconds and then serve the pineapple straight from the pan with the juices spooned over.

# Pineapple Upside-Down Pudding

*This is a good winter pudding to follow a light main course.*

**Topping:**
1 oz (25 g) butter
1 oz (25 g) light soft brown
  sugar
4 slices fresh pineapple

**Pudding:**
4 oz (100 g) self-raising flour
1 level teaspoon baking powder
1 level teaspoon cinnamon
4 oz (100 g) soft margarine
4 oz (100 g) light soft brown
  sugar
2 eggs

Heat the oven to 350 °F, 180 °C, gas mark 4. Grease a 7 inch (17.5 cm) square tin and line with a piece of greaseproof paper.

Cream the butter and sugar together and spread over the base of the tin. Remove the skin from the pineapple and cut the core from the centre and place the slices in the tin on top of the creamed topping.

To make the pudding: place all the ingredients in a bowl and beat well for a few minutes until they are blended. Spread over the pineapple and smooth the surface.

Bake in the oven for about 40 minutes or until the pudding is well risen and golden brown and has shrunk slightly from the sides of the tin.

Turn out on to a warm serving dish and serve with custard or ice cream.

# Plum

Plums are home grown or imported, dessert or culinary, yellow, red, green, purple or black. In fact, they are a versatile fruit. Some of the best eating varieties are grown in the South and the Midlands of England, notably the Victoria – straight from the tree it is equal for flavour and sweetness with the peach. While the season for the best home-grown fruit is limited to late summer, imported plums are available from January until September.

Dessert plums should be firm to the touch, with a bloom on the skin. Fresh ripe fruit can be stored for two or three days – not longer – in a cool place. Cooking plums are stewed, used in pies, tarts and puddings. They make good jam. To prepare plums, wash them and remove the stones. Crack some of the stones and cook the kernels with the fruit to enhance the flavour.

Plums can be frozen, in syrup or stewed, as for greengages.

# Roast Chicken with Plum Stuffing

Serves 4

*You can substitute damsons for plums – but do not be tempted to try greengages as they do not give the necessary colour to the stuffing.*

3½ lb (1.6 kg) roasting chicken
1 oz (25 g) butter
8 plums

*Stuffing:*
4 oz (100 g) fresh white
  breadcrumbs
1 oz (25 g) walnuts, roughly
  chopped
2 red plums, stoned
  and chopped
1 tablespoon chopped fresh
  parsley
1 egg
salt and pepper

Heat the oven to 400 °F, 200 °C, gas mark 6.

Mix all the stuffing ingredients together and stuff into the neck end of the chicken.

Place the chicken in a roasting tin. Spread the breast with butter and roast in the oven for 1½ hours or until the chicken is golden brown and tender. Remove the chicken from the oven 15 minutes before the end of cooking time and strain any excess fat from the roasting tin. Put in the plums and return to the oven for 15 minutes.

Arrange the chicken on a serving dish and place the plums around. Serve 2 plums with each portion of chicken.

# Crunchy Plum Betsie

Serves 4 to 6

*This is a crumble with a difference. The rolled oats give it an extra crumbly and crunchy texture.*

1½ lb (675 g) plums, greengages
  or damsons
2 oz granulated sugar
2 oz (50 g) plain flour

2 oz (50 g) rolled oats
3 oz (75 g) demerara sugar
2 oz (50 g) soft margarine

Heat the oven to 400 °F, 200 °C, gas mark 6.

Wash, stone and quarter the plums and place them in an ovenproof dish. Sprinkle over the granulated sugar and put the dish into the oven.

Mix togther the flour, oats and sugar and rub in the margarine.

Take the plums from the oven and give them a stir, then make sure that they are level in the dish and sprinkle the oat mixture over the top. Lightly press this down and then bake in the oven for 45 minutes.

Serve warm with cream or ice cream.

# Plum and Almond Tart                              Serves 6

*If plums are not available you could use apricots, greengages or pears; use just sufficient fruit to make a single layer in the base of the flan.*

**Pastry:**
6 oz (175 g) plain flour
1½ oz (40 g) margarine
1½ oz (40 g) lard
about 6 teaspoons cold water to mix

**Filling:**
5 red plums
4 oz (100 g) butter
4 oz (100 g) caster sugar
1 egg, beaten
4 oz (100 g) ground rice
½ teaspoon almond essence

Heat the oven to 400 °F, 200 °C, gas mark 6.

Make the pastry in the usual way (see Deep Apple Pie, page 20). Roll it out on a floured surface and line an 8 inch (20 cm) flan ring, which should be placed on a baking sheet. Prick the base with a fork. Leave the pastry to rest in the refrigerator for 10 minutes.

Cut the plums in half, remove the stones and place, cut side down, in the flan. Heat the butter in a saucepan until it has just melted but is not brown. Stir in the sugar and cook for a minute, remove from heat and add the egg, ground rice and almond essence. Pour this mixture over the plums. If liked, any pastry trimmings may be rolled out, cut in strips and arranged in a lattice on top of the tart.

Bake in the oven for 35 to 40 minutes until the filling is risen and golden brown; it should spring back when lightly pressed with the finger.

Take the tart from the oven and leave to cool.

# Plum Crisp

Serves 4

*This is quite a filling pudding. The ground rice gives a very good texture and crunchiness. If you have no ground rice, try semolina.*

4 oz (100 g) plain flour
2 oz (50 g) ground rice
3 oz (75 g) caster sugar
4 oz (100 g) butter

2 oz (50 g) cake crumbs
1 level teaspoon ground ginger
1 lb (450 g) red plums

Heat the oven to 400 °F, 200 °C, gas mark 6. Butter an ovenproof dish measuring about 11 by 6 inches (27.5 by 15 cm).

Put the flour, ground rice and sugar in a bowl and add the butter, cut into small pieces, and rub in with the fingertips until the mixture resembles fine breadcrumbs. Press over the base of the dish.

Mix the cake crumbs with the ginger and sprinkle over the base.

Cut the plums in half, remove the stones and arrange, cut side down, in the dish.

Bake in the oven for about 50 minutes until the plums are soft and the base is crisp and a pale golden brown. Serve warm with custard.

# Pomegranate

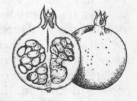

The pomegranate is roughly the size of an orange, with a thin, but tough, smooth skin. When ripe the skin is pink or red, and the fruit is divided into segments and full of seeds which are surrounded by the pulpy flesh. It is in season from September to January and most of the pomegranates sold in Britain are imported from the Mediterranean countries.

Eat the fruit raw, sucking the flesh from the seeds, or crush the flesh to extract the juice to add to fruit salads or drinks.

# Quince

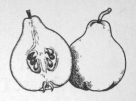

The quince is similar to the japonica, but larger. It is apple- or pear-shaped, with a yellow or russet skin that is covered with a light fuzz when ripe. The flesh is hard and sour and there are a lot of seeds.

Quinces are sometimes available in the shops during October and November, but most nowadays are home grown. They can be stewed but are most often used in marmalade, jam and jelly.

## Quince Jelly

*A few spoonfuls of quince jelly can be used to sweeten stewed apples.*

2 lb (900 g) quinces
3 pints (1.7 litres) water

2 level teaspoons citric acid
granulated sugar

Wash and cut up the quinces. Place them in a saucepan with the water and citric acid, cover and cook gently for about 1 hour or until the fruit is tender.

Strain through a jelly bag, leaving overnight if possible.

To each pint (600 ml) of quince juice allow 1 lb (450 g) granulated sugar. Put the juice and the sugar in a saucepan and heat through until the sugar has dissolved, then boil rapidly until setting point is reached. (See Crab Apple Jelly, page 61.)

Pot in clean warm jars, label and seal.

# Raspberry

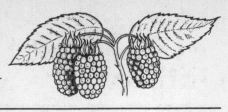

Raspberries are one of the glories of our summer. They are little trouble to grow and most gardens can find room for a row or two of the canes. Commercially, they are grown all over Britain, particularly in Scotland, where much of our finest soft fruit is produced.

Raspberries are easy to eat, as a dessert with sugar or cream, in sweets, in tarts, in jam, or added to home-made yogurt. Eat them as soon as possible after picking – no problem this – as they are perishable and easily damaged. Wash and handle them as little as possible. When bought, they come already hulled and all you have to do is look them over and discard any that show signs of mildew or mould.

The summer crop is at its best during July and August. A second later variety is available in the autumn.

Raspberries can be bottled and canned and they freeze very well indeed. They may be dry frozen whole, or frozen as a purée. A lot of growers run pick-your-own schemes at the height of the season. Take advantage of these offers if you can; pick a good supply of raspberries and freeze enough to bring the taste of summer to your table throughout the rest of the year.

# Raspberry Cream

Serves 4 to 6

*To make this recipe more economical, use a small tin of evaporated milk, well chilled before whipping, instead of cream.*

1 packet raspberry jelly
½ pint (300 ml) boiling water

½ pint (300 ml) whipping cream
8 oz (225 g) raspberries

Break the jelly into cubes and dissolve them in the boiling water. Leave on one side until the jelly begins to thicken and set.

Whip the cream until it forms soft peaks. Sieve the raspberries, reserving a few for decoration.

Fold the jelly into the cream, together with the raspberry purée and turn into a glass serving dish. Leave in a cool place to set and then decorate with a few raspberries.

# Raspberry Kissel

Serves 4

*This is a Danish recipe. You can substitute red currants for raspberries if you wish.*

2 level tablespoons cornflour
¼ level teaspoon ground
   cinnamon
1 rounded tablespoon
   granulated sugar

¼ pint (150 ml) water
1 orange
8 oz (225 g) raspberries
caster sugar

Place the cornflour, cinnamon and sugar in a saucepan, blend the water in gradually and bring to the boil, stirring continuously until the mixture has thickened. Simmer for 1 minute.

Grate the rind and squeeze the juice from the orange and add both to the saucepan. Stir in the raspberries. Taste and, if liked, add a little more sugar. Divide the mixture between 4 small glasses or individual dishes and sprinkle over the caster sugar – this will prevent a skin forming. Leave to cool.

Serve with small crisp biscuits or shortbread.

# Raspberry Sorbet

Serves 8

*Raspberries and lemons are thought to make the best sorbets. However gooseberries have an intriguing flavour – choose young fruit and cook in a minimal amount of water with 3 oz (75 g) granulated sugar and then purée them.*

1 lb (450 g) raspberries
6 oz (175 g) sugar
½ pint (300 ml) water

juice of 1 orange
3 egg whites

Purée the raspberries in a blender and then pass them through a sieve and discard all the pips.

Put the sugar and water together in a pan and heat gently until the sugar has dissolved, then bring to the boil and simmer for 5 minutes. Remove from the heat and stir in the raspberry purée and orange juice. Pour the mixture into a bowl and, when it is cool, put it into a 3½ pint (2 litre) container. Place it in the freezer and leave until partially frozen.

Whisk the egg whites until they are stiff and then whisk in the partially frozen purée, a tablespoonful at a time. Return the mixture to the container, cover, label and freeze.

Serve in scoops in glasses accompanied by a crisp wafer biscuit. The sorbets look lovely decorated with a whole fresh raspberry and perhaps a small sprig of mint.

# Raspberry Syllabub

Serves 4 to 6

*This is a delicious summer pudding, and very quick to make.*

1 lb (450 g) fresh raspberries
about 2 oz (50 g) icing cream
½ pint (300 ml) double cream

2 tablespoons Kirsch or brandy
small sprigs of fresh mint

Put a few raspberries on one side for decoration. Reduce the remainder to a purée in an electric blender with the icing sugar, then sieve to remove all the pips. Alternatively just sieve the raspberries together with the icing sugar.

Whisk the double cream until thick, fold in the raspberry purée and add Kirsch or brandy if liked.

Turn into tall glasses and decorate with the reserved raspberries and sprigs of fresh mint.

# Raspberry Queen of Puddings

Serves 6 to 8

*Raspberries or loganberries have a fine strong flavour for this recipe but you could use very ripe strawberries, with a little lemon juice added.*

| | |
|---|---|
| 1 pint (600 ml) milk | *Topping:* |
| 1 oz (25 g) butter | 4 egg whites |
| 2 oz (50 g) caster sugar | 8 oz (225 g) caster sugar |
| finely grated rind of 1 lemon | |
| 4 egg yolks | |
| 3 oz (75 g) fresh white breadcrumbs | |
| 4 oz (100 g) raspberries | |

Heat the oven to 350°F, 180°C, gas mark 4. Grease a 2 pint (1 litre) ovenproof dish.

Warm the milk in a small saucepan, then add the butter, sugar and lemon rind. Stir lightly so that the sugar dissolves and the butter melts. Whisk the egg yolks in a small bowl and gradually whisk in the warmed milk. Put the breadcrumbs in the dish and pour the warm milk over them. Leave to stand for about 15 minutes, then bake in the oven for 25 minutes or until just set.

Remove the dish from the oven. Mash the raspberries and, if liked, sweeten them with a little sugar and then spread them over the warm custard.

Whisk the egg whites until they are stiff and whisk in the sugar a teaspoonful at a time. Pile the egg whites on top of the pudding, spreading them right to the edge of the dish so that the custard is completely covered and spoon into rough peaks.

Return the dish to the oven and bake for a further 10 to 15 minutes until the meringue is just tinged a pale golden brown all over. Serve at once.

# Rhubarb

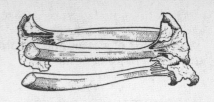

Rhubarb is a bit of a contradiction: strictly speaking a vegetable, it is normally classed and used as a fruit. The leaves are highly poisonous. You can eat the stem, but it must be cooked, preferably with a lot of sugar.

Rhubarb makes an excellent full-flavoured filling for tarts and pies. It is also used in jam or marmalade with the addition of ginger. It makes good chutney, too. Add a proportion of rhubarb to an apple chutney recipe or interchange the two.

There are two kinds of rhubarb. The forced variety, grown largely in the north of England, is a pinkish colour with delicately flavoured stalks, available from December to mid-April. Home grown outdoor rhubarb (March to June) is more robust, with tougher, thicker stalks, dark red in colour, and with a stronger flavour. Outdoor rhubarb is generally preferred for pies and tarts. This variety is frequently grown in country gardens with an old bucket on top to bring it along.

Don't buy rhubarb if it has limp stalks. For cooking, trim the ends, then swash the stalks and cut into cubes. Do not forget the sugar.

Rhubarb can be frozen, plain or in syrup.

# Hot Rhubarb and Orange

Serves 6

*This is also very good served cold with a dollop of whipped cream.*

2 lb (900 g) rhubarb
8 oz (225 g) granulated sugar

2 rounded tablespoons orange
   marmalade
¼ pint (150 ml) boiling water

Heat the oven to 325 °F, 160 °C, gas mark 3.

Wash the rhubarb and cut into neat 1 inch (2.5 cm) lengths and place in an ovenproof dish, together with the sugar, marmalade and water. Cover and cook for about 45 to 60 minutes. The time will vary with the age and thickness of the rhubarb, which should be quite tender but still have kept a perfect shape.

# Rhubarb and Ginger Fool

Serves 4 to 6

*Guests often taste the ginger in this but are at a loss to know what the fruit is. It is very good served with shortbread fingers.*

1 lb (450 g) rhubarb
4 oz (100 g) demerara sugar
finely grated rind and juice of 1
   small orange

small piece of root ginger
¼ pint (150 ml) double cream,
   lightly whipped

Cut the rhubarb into 2 inch (5 cm) lengths and place in a saucepan with the sugar and orange rind and juice. Place the pan over a moderate heat and stir occasionally until the sugar has dissolved. Then add the piece of root ginger and simmer the rhubarb gently until tender – this will take about 10 to 15 minutes. Lift out the piece of ginger and purée the fruit in the blender until it is smooth. Leave on one side, in a bowl, to cool.

When quite cold, stir in the cream until the mixture is blended evenly and then turn into a glass serving dish and chill in the refrigerator until it is required.

# Summer Pudding

Serves 4 to 6

*The fruit filling for this pudding is delicious served on its own, very cold, with plain yogurt.*

6 to 8 large, fairly thin, slices white bread, with the crusts removed
8 oz (225 g) rhubarb
8 oz (225 g) mixed currants black, red and white

8 oz (225 g) granulated sugar
6 tablespoons water
8 oz (225 g) small strawberries, or large ones halved
8 oz (225 g) loganberries

Put 1 slice of bread on one side for the top; use the remainder to line the base and sides of a 2 pint (1 litre) round, fairly shallow, dish.

Put the rhubarb, cut into ½ inch (1.25 cm) slices, with the currants, in a saucepan. Add the sugar and water, bring to the boil and simmer, stirring frequently, for a few minutes until the fruit is barely tender. Add the strawberries and loganberries and cook for a further minute.

Turn the mixture into the dish, place the slice of bread on top and bend over the tops of the sliced bread at the sides towards the centre. Put a saucer on top, pressing it down a little until the juice rises to the top of the dish. Leave to soak overnight in the refrigerator.

Turn out just before serving and serve with lots of cream.


# Children's Rhubarb Fool

Serves 4

*My children love this. I also make it with other fruit purées, and it is particularly good made with gooseberries, with a little green colouring added. Add the ice cream just before serving.*

1 lb (450 g) young rhubarb
2 tablespoons water
3 to 4 oz (75 to 100 g) caster sugar

17 fl oz (510 ml) family brick vanilla ice cream
a little pink colouring

Place the rhubarb, cut into short lengths, in a saucepan with the water. Cover and cook gently until the rhubarb is tender, this will take about 10 to 15 minutes. Remove from the heat and sieve into a bowl. Add the sugar and leave to become quite cold.

Remove the ice cream from the freezer and leave to soften at room temperature for about 10 minutes. Stir the ice cream into the purée and mix until well blended; if liked add a few drops of pink colouring.

Turn the fool into a glass dish and serve with shortbread biscuits.

# Rosy Red Fruit Pie                                   Serves 4 to 6

*If you prefer, make this as a crumble rather than a pie. Omit the water from the pastry mix and, of course, you will not need milk to glaze or a pie funnel. Make sure the fruit is well packed down before topping with the crumble.*

| | |
|---|---|
| 8 oz (225 g) rhubarb | **Pastry:** |
| 4 oz (100 g) bilberries | 6 oz (175 g) plain flour |
| 8 oz (225 g) cherries | 1½ oz (40 g) margarine |
| 4 oz (100 g) black currants, or | 1½ oz (40 g) lard |
| red currants if available | about 6 teaspoons cold water |
| 3 oz (75 g) caster sugar | milk to glaze |
| 2 tablespoons cold water | granulated sugar |

Put a pie funnel in the centre of a 1½ pint (900 ml) pie dish. Cut the rhubarb into 1 inch (2.5 cm) lengths and mix with all the other fruits; put half in the base of the pie dish and then sprinkle with the sugar and cover with the remaining fruit. Add about 2 tablespoons water.

Make the pastry (see Deep Apple Pie, page 20) and then roll out on a floured surface and use to cover the top of the pie dish: use any trimmings to decorate if liked. Chill in the refrigerator for 30 minutes.

Heat the oven to 400°F, 200°C, gas mark 6. Brush the pastry with milk and sprinkle with sugar; make a small slit in the centre for the steam to escape. Bake in the oven for 40 to 45 minutes until the fruit is tender and the pastry crisp and a pale golden brown.

# Rhubarb and Apple Chutney   Makes about 9 lb (4 kg)

*If windfall apples and late summer rhubarb are used, this chutney will be very inexpensive to make. Chutneys are best potted in clear glass jars, and labelled with the date of making, the variety of chutney and whether it is mild or hot. Chutneys are an invaluable part of the store cupboard. They mellow and improve with keeping and should be stored for at least six to eight weeks before eating.*

3½ lb (1.6 kg) cooking apples
1½ pints (900 ml) malt vinegar
1 lb (450 g) rhubarb, chopped
8 oz (225 g) stoned dates
1 oz (25 g) pickling spice

1 level teaspoon ground ginger
1 level teaspoon mixed spice
2 level tablespoons salt
2 lb (900 g) dark soft brown sugar

Wash and chop the apples and put them in a saucepan with the vinegar. Cover and simmer for 20 minutes until soft and pulpy. Rub the apples through a sieve to separate the pips, cores and peel from the fruit pulp. Rinse out the saucepan.

Return the apple purée to the saucepan, add the rhubarb and dates and simmer for 20 minutes.

Meanwhile, grind the pickling spice in a pepper mill or electric grinder, or place in a thick polythene bag and crush with a hammer.

Add the ground spice, together with all the remaining ingredients, to the saucepan and simmer for 20 minutes.

Pot and cover while very hot with plastic or screw top vinegar-proof lids.

# Sloe

The sloe is the fruit of the blackthorn which whitens our hedgerows in early spring. The fruits appear in late summer, resembling very small round plums, dark-purple or black in colour with a blue bloom. They are extremely sour.

Choose firm, blemish-free fruit and store in a cool place. They can be frozen dry.

## Sloe Gin

*If you can find sloes and afford gin, this works out cheaper than other liqueurs. Little bottles filled with sloe gin make excellent Christmas presents. It is very, very good! Gauge the quantity of sloes, gin and sugar required according to the size of your bottles and the amount of sloes you have.*

Wash the sloes, remove the stalks and snip each sloe with scissors or a sharp knife.

Take a clean empty gin bottle, or similar, and fill two-thirds full with snipped sloes. To each bottle add 6 to 8 oz (175 g to 225 g) caster sugar and then fill the bottle up with gin. Put the lid on and shake the bottle very well.

Put on one side on the larder shelf for at least 2 months before using, shaking the bottle about twice a week. In theory you should not drink it for at least 6 months, but in practice you will find that you are unable to wait that long. Serve, in small glasses, as an after-dinner drink. After 6 months the gin should be strained off the sloes, which should then be discarded.

# Strawberry

The present vogue for nostalgia in plays, books and television looks back to bright, imagined, sunlit days – tea on the lawn with cucumber sandwiches, strawberries and cream. Well, we still have the strawberries, better than ever, perhaps, juicier, sweeter and more succulent, thanks to modern growing methods. The strawberry is *the* summer fruit – during the Wimbledon fortnight newspapers provide statistics of the amount of strawberries eaten around the tennis courts.

The strawberry is at its supreme best as a dessert fruit. It needs little dressing up. Just hull the berries and pile them in a large dish. With sugar, of course, and cream certainly. Some people believe that a shake of pepper enhances the flavour, but you hardly need such additions. Picked straight from the plant, still warm from the sun, the essential strawberry asks for no outside help.

There are innumerable strawberry recipes – jelly, mousse, fool, ice cream, meringue, strawberry shortcake for a special occasion – the list is endless. They are simply delicious served in cider, brandy or white wine: marinate the fruit in brandy and sugar and, just before serving, add some really cold bubbly cider. Use strawberries fresh in tarts, and use the smaller, less perfect berries for cooking. There are special varieties for jam-making.

The height of the season is from the end of May until July and there is another smaller crop in the autumn. The fruit is grown throughout Britain, some of the best, like raspberries, coming from Scotland. Do not forget the pick-your-own offers made by many growers who are finding fruit harvesting for the commercial market prohibitively expensive.

Strawberries freeze best as a purée. If you do not want to spend precious summer days making jam, freeze a supply of suitable berries and turn them into jam later.

**Recipes:**

Other recipes using
strawberries:
Avocado and Strawberry Mille
Feuille, 44
Glazed Fruit Flan, 83
Strawberry Ice Cream, 192
Summer Pudding, 160

See also:
Apple Cinnamon Shortcake, 24
Black Cherry Cheesecake, 57
Lemon Pavlova with Kiwi Fruit,
99
Quick Fruit Brûlée, 133
Raspberry Queen of Puddings,
157

# Strawberry Soufflé.

Serves 4

*Try this recipe with a mixture of strawberries and raspberries, or raspberries alone.*

8 oz (225 g) fresh strawberries
3 eggs, separated
2 oz (50 g) caster sugar
2 tablespoons orange or lemon
juice

2 level teaspoons gelatine
2 tablespoons water
¼ pint (150 ml) whipping cream
few small strawberries, to
decorate

Place a band of non-stick silicone paper around a 1½ pint (900 ml) soufflé dish to come 2 inches (5 cm) above the rim. (See Chilled Apricot Soufflé, page 35).

Hull the strawberries and mash them well. In a bowl put the egg yolks, sugar and orange or lemon juice and stand it over a pan of hot water. Whisk until the mixture is thick and will leave a trail.

Place the gelatine and water in a small cup or bowl and stand it in a pan of simmering water until the gelatine is dissolved and clear. Remove, cool slightly and then whisk into the egg-yolk mixture, together with the mashed strawberries. Leave on one side until it is beginning to set.

Whisk the egg whites until they are stiff and then whisk the cream until it forms soft peaks. Fold the cream into the strawberry mixture and, lastly, carefully fold in the egg white.

Turn the mixture into the prepared dish and chill in the refrigerator until firm. Remove the paper and decorate the top with a few small strawberries and then serve with shortbread fingers.

# Strawberry Torte

Serves 8

*This recipe makes a rather small amount of strawberries go a long way. It is just the thing to produce at the beginning of the season when strawberries are few and far between.*

**Base:**
3 oz (75 g) hazelnuts
7½ oz (212 g) plain flour
4½ oz (125 g) butter
3 oz (75 g) caster sugar

**Filling:**
12 oz (350 g) strawberries
½ pint (300 ml) whipping
   cream

Heat the oven to 375 °F, 190 °C, gas mark 5. Lightly grease 3 baking sheets.

Take the rack from the grill pan, put in the hazelnuts and grill them lightly for 2 to 3 minutes. Rub the nuts between 2 sheets of kitchen paper or in a clean tea towel to remove all the skins and then chop.

Put the flour in a bowl, rub in the butter until the mixture resembles fine breadcrumbs, stir in the nuts and sugar and then knead well together to form a firm dough.

Divide the mixture into 3 and press each portion out on the baking sheets to form a 7 inch (17.5 cm) circle. Bake them in the oven for 15 minutes, then leave to cool slightly on the baking sheet before lifting them off and cooling them on a wire rack.

Hull the strawberries and cut each in half lengthwise. Whisk the cream until it thickens and forms peaks. Place a small quantity on one side and mix half of the strawberries with the rest of the cream.

Put one layer of the torte on a serving dish and cover with half the strawberry cream. Place another layer on top and cover with the remaining strawberry cream. Place the final torte on top, cover with strawberries and place a spoonful of cream in the centre. Leave for at least an hour before serving.

# Strawberry Whip                              Serves 8

*This is a superb sweet – it makes a few strawberries go a very long way. It works very well with raspberries, too.*

8 oz (225 g) strawberries          3 oz (75 g) icing sugar,
1 egg white                                  sieved

Wipe the strawberries and hull them; do not wash the fruit as it is important that it is dry.

Put the strawberries in a bowl and mash well – a stainless steel potato masher works very well. Mix in the egg white and icing sugar and with an electric hand whisk, beat well for about 10 minutes or until the mixture is very thick and creamy. If using a hand rotary whisk this will take longer and if using an electric mixer on top speed the mixture will be ready in about 5 to 6 minutes.

Turn into a glass serving dish and chill for 1 or 2 hours and then serve decorated with whole strawberries. If liked, the mixture may be served individually in glasses.

# Fresh Strawberry Sauce                    Serves 6 to 8

*This is delicious poured over ice cream. Puréed strawberries take up less room in the freezer than whole ones.*

1 lb (450 g) fresh strawberries,    7 oz (200 g) caster sugar
  or frozen may be used               juice of 1 lemon

Put the hulled strawberries, sugar and lemon juice in a blender. If using frozen fruit allow it to thaw first. Cover the blender and run until the strawberries are puréed.

Turn the purée into a serving dish, cover and chill in the refrigerator until required.

# Tangerine, Mandarin and Satsuma

The tangerine family has grown over the years as new varieties have joined it. Once tangerines arrived at Christmas in flat wooden boxes, every other fruit wrapped in silver paper. Now you go to the greengrocer and buy them by the pound, specifying which of the different types you want.

The **tangerine** is a small sweet type of orange with a flavour of its own. It has a loose, bright orange skin, small juicy segments and usually a lot of pips. It is imported from Morocco and Spain, from September to March.

The **mandarin** is very similar to the tangerine and is a popular Christmas dessert fruit. It has a loose oily skin, pinkish-yellow flesh and some pips. It comes from Italy, Spain and Morocco, from October to March. This is the kind that is so popular in cans.

The **satsuma** has largely supplanted the tangerine and mandarin; its big advantage is that it has no pips. It comes from Spain and Morocco, from October to February.

All the varieties of the tangerine family are eaten fresh as dessert fruit. They can be used for marmalade, alone or mixed with other citrus fruits.

Store and freeze in the same way as oranges.

# Cottage Cheese and Satsuma Salad

Serves 4

*This is a particularly good salad for slimmers – no dressing is required.*

| | |
|---|---|
| 1 small lettuce | 4 oz (100 g) green grapes |
| 8 oz (225 g) carton cottage cheese | 4 oz (100 g) black grapes |
| | ½ small cucumber |
| 3 satsumas | a bunch of watercress |

Wash the lettuce, drain well and then arrange on a large flat dish. Pile the cottage cheese in the centre.

Peel the satsumas and remove any pith. Cut the grapes in half and remove the pips. Arrange the halved grapes with the satsumas on each lettuce leaf. Slice the cucumber and arrange it in a circle around the cottage cheese. Garnish the dish with small sprigs of watercress.

# Tangerine Syllabub

Serves 4

*This recipe is also good with limes instead of tangerines; leave out the lemon juice and add the grated rind and juice of 3 limes.*

| | |
|---|---|
| 6 tangerines | 2 oz (50 g) demerara sugar |
| 2 tablespoons lemon juice | ½ pint (300 ml) double cream |

Peel 3 of the tangerines, pull apart the segments and remove any pith which surrounds them. Halve and squeeze the juice from the remaining tangerines.

Add the lemon juice and sugar to the tangerine juice and heat gently over a low heat until the sugar has dissolved. Remove from the heat and leave to cool.

Whisk the cream until it is thick and then gradually whisk in the cooled juices. Divide half the segments between 4 glasses and spoon the cream mixture on top. Decorate with the remaining tangerine segments.

Chill in the refrigerator before serving, accompanied by sponge or shortbread fingers.

# Satsuma and
# Seville Marmalade

Makes about 10 lb (4.5 kg)

*Satsumas and tangerines do not contain enough acid or pectin to make a well-set marmalade, but if they are combined with Seville oranges or lemons then a good result can be obtained.*

2 lb (900 g) satsumas
1½ lb (675 g) Seville oranges
juice of 2 lemons

scant 2½ pints (1.4 litres) water
6 lb (2.7 kg) granulated sugar

Put the washed, whole unpeeled fruit, lemon juice and water in a pressure cooker and cook for 40 minutes. Alternatively place the fruit in a saucepan with a tight-fitting lid and simmer for 2 to 2½ hours until the fruit skins are really soft. There should be 1 to 1½ pints (600 to 900 ml) of liquid in the pan. The fruit should pierce easily with a fork and disintegrate if pinched firmly.

Allow the fruit to cool, then remove from the saucepan and cut into quarters. Take out all the pips and add these to the liquid in the saucepan and simmer for 15 minutes.

Meanwhile, finely shred the fruit with a stainless steel knife. Put into a bowl and strain on the juice from the pips. Discard the pips and return the fruit, peel, pulp and juice to the saucepan. Add the sugar and stir well to dissolve. Bring to the boil. Remove any scum which rises to the surface with a slotted spoon. Boil rapidly, stirring occasionally, for about 20 minutes until the marmalade has reached setting point. (See Crab Apple Jelly, page 61.)

Remove the saucepan from the heat and leave the marmalade to cool for about 5 minutes so that the peel will be evenly suspended in the jars.

Pot into clean, warm jars and cover with waxed paper, wax side down. Leave until cold. Finally, cover the pots with cellophane covers and screwtops, or snap-on plastic lids.

# Ugli

This extraordinary looking fruit, which it must be admitted seems to be well named, comes from Jamaica. It is far from beautiful, looking as it does like a misshapen grapefruit with a thick knobbly skin. In fact it tastes quite delicious, something like a cross between a grapefruit and a tangerine, but sweeter. The yellow or pink flesh is very juicy and has few pips.

The season is from October to February but the ugli, or tangelo as it is sometimes called, is often in short supply. Specialist greengrocers or fruit shops are your best bet – and it is worth eating if you can track it down.

Eat the ugli raw for dessert or use in any recipes that specify oranges.

It can be frozen whole or divided into segments for up to three months.

**For recipes using uglis, see Orange**

# NUTS

# Almond

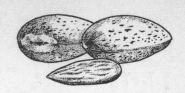

The almond is the fruit of a small flowering tree that flourishes in such warm temperate countries as Spain and Italy. It is the same tree that brings a welcome touch of colour in early spring to gardens and city squares in the south of England. This English almond is strictly decorative – its fruit is not for eating.

There are two main varieties. Bitter almonds are inedible and are used for flavouring only – one almond will flavour a whole dish – and are made into almond essence and oil. If you are using almond essence to accentuate the taste of almonds in cooking, be careful, it is very strong.

Sweet almonds are the ones we eat and enjoy in different forms. Buy them in the shell at Christmas time when they are at their best. Mix them with other nuts for a decorative effect. Shelled almonds are available in supermarkets and health food stores all the year round. Blanched almonds have had their papery skins removed. Use them as decoration for cakes and trifles, or fried in butter and sprinkled with salt as a garnish, or for nibbling with drinks.

Ground almonds, well known as the main ingredient of marzipan, are simply blanched almonds reduced to a fine consistency. You can do this yourself in a blender or coffee grinder. Use them for almond-flavoured cakes and biscuits, macaroons and puddings.

The almond, like most nuts, stores well in an airtight container. In their shells they will keep indefinitely in the freezer – even shelled ones freeze for up to five years, ground up to one year. A good tip is to put different nuts in individual bags and store the lot in one big polythene bag, where you can get at them easily. After all, you do not want to have to dash out to the shops every time the recipe calls for a small quantity of blanched almonds.

Recipes:

Other recipes using almonds:
Apple Strudel, 19
Black Currant Griestorte, 68
Pear and Ginger Trifle, 137

See also:
Buttered Brazils, 177
Hazelnut Biscuits, 180

# Grilled Sole with Buttered Almonds

Serves 2

*Dover sole is so rare and expensive these days that this is a special recipe for a special occasion. In my opinion Dover sole should always be kept on the bone.*

2 Dover soles, each about 8 oz
(225 g) in weight
1½ oz (40 g) butter
salt and pepper
1 tablespoon oil

1 oz (25 g) blanched almonds,
split
2 bananas, peeled and sliced
2 tablespoons brandy
lemon wedges and watercress
sprigs to garnish

Ask your fishmonger to remove the skin from the soles. Place the soles on the rack in a grill pan, dot them with 1 oz (25 g) of the butter and season well with salt and pepper. Grill the soles for about 10 minutes, turning once. When the soles have been turned, spoon the butter in the bottom of the grill pan over them and sprinkle each with a little more salt and pepper. Grill until the skin is white all through – test at the thickest part of the backbone with the point of a knife.

Meanwhile, melt the remaining butter and oil in a small frying pan and fry the almonds until they are golden brown.

Draw the pan to one side, add the bananas and fry them until they are just turning colour. Pour in the brandy, warm it slightly over a low heat and then set light to it.

When the soles are cooked, arrange them on a serving dish and scatter the almonds and banana slices on top.

Garnish with lemon wedges and watercress.

# Almond, Chicken and Rice Salad

Serves 6

*Assemble this salad about 6 hours before you need it, but only add the peas at the very last moment, otherwise they will lose their colour. If you prefer, instead of the peas, use chopped red and yellow peppers.*

3 lb (1.4 kg) cooked chicken
8 oz (225 g) long-grain rice
8 oz (225 g) fresh pineapple diced
2 oz (50 g) seedless raisins
2 spring onions, chopped
4 oz (100 g) button mushrooms
1 oz (25 g) butter
2 oz (50 g) flaked almonds
8 oz (225 g) packet frozen peas, cooked

*Dressing:*
2 level teaspoons caster sugar
3 level teaspoons salt
1 teaspoon made mustard
freshly ground black pepper
6 tablespoons oil
2 tablespoons white wine vinegar

Remove the meat from the chicken and cut it into small pieces.

Bring a large pan of water to the boil and cook the rice, with plenty of salt, until it is tender (this usually takes about 12 minutes or as directed on the packet). Drain very thoroughly and rinse in warm water to get rid of all excess starch. Turn it into a large bowl.

Add the chicken, pineapple, raisins and spring onions to the rice.

Pour boiling water over the button mushrooms and leave to stand for 5 minutes. Then drain them well, finely slice them, and add them to the rice mixture.

Put the sugar, salt, mustard, pepper, oil and vinegar in a bowl and whisk together until blended. Stir into the rice and mix very well; taste and check seasoning.

Melt the butter in a small saucepan and fry the almonds until they are golden brown; then lift them out and leave to cool.

Cover the salad with pieces of foil or cling film and chill in the refrigerator for several hours to allow the flavours to blend.

When required, again taste and check seasoning, turn in the peas and pile the mixture on to a large serving dish.

Scatter the almonds over and serve.

# Almond Paste

Makes enough to cover an 8 inch (20 cm) round cake

*Almond paste keeps well in the refrigerator, but it should be taken out of the refrigerator, allowed to stand in a warm room and then kneaded before being used to top a cake. Use any leftover remains to stuff dates.*

6 oz (175 g) icing sugar
6 oz (175 g) ground almonds
6 oz (175 g) caster sugar

3 egg yolks, lightly beaten
almond essence
juice of half a lemon

Sift the icing sugar into a bowl, add the ground almonds and sugar and mix well. Add the egg yolks, then the almond essence and then the lemon juice. Work the mixture into a small, smooth ball by hand but do not over-knead.

# Salted Almonds

Home-made salted almonds are so much nicer than the bought variety. To make them yourself, blanch almonds in boiling water until the skin slips off easily, then drain and fry them in a little butter and oil until they are a pale gold. Drain them on kitchen paper and then sprinkle with salt.

# Brazil Nut

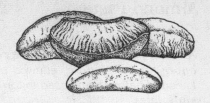

Brazil nuts, sometimes called the almonds of the Amazon, grow in a large woody shell, something like a coconut. Inside the shell, packed like the segments of an orange, are 18 to 24 of the triangular shaped nuts that we are familiar with in the shops. Each nut has its own very hard shell and a sweet, white, creamy kernel.

Brazil nuts are plentiful around Christmas and it is worth buying them in bulk because they store well in polythene bags in a cool cupboard, or shelled in the freezer.

It is difficult to crack the shells without spoiling the kernel, so if a recipe calls for whole nuts, buy them ready shelled. The shelled weight of the nuts is about half the unshelled weight.

Recipes:
Brazil Nut and Cheese Loaf, 176    Buttered Brazils, 177

## Brazil Nut and Cheese Loaf

*A deliciously different, and very nutritious, bread to add to a packed lunch, or use to make toasted sandwiches or a base for scrambled egg.*

8 oz (225 g) plain flour
2 level tablespoons baking
  powder
1 level teaspoon dry mustard
1 level teaspoon salt
½ level teaspoon ground black
  pepper

3 oz (75 g) butter
4 oz (100 g) Cheddar cheese,
  grated
2 oz (50 g) Brazil nuts, chopped
2 large eggs
¼ pint (150 ml) milk

Heat the oven to 350 °F, 180 °C, gas mark 4. Well grease a 1 lb (450 g) loaf tin.

Put the flour in a large bowl, together with the baking powder, mustard and seasoning. Add the butter, cut into small pieces, and rub it in with the fingertips until the mixture resembles breadcrumbs. Then stir in the cheese and nuts. Beat the egg and milk together, stir into the dry ingredients and mix well to make a stiff dough.

Turn the dough into the loaf tin and bake in the oven for 1 hour. Turn out and leave to cool on a wire rack.

Serve, cut in slices, either cold or toasted..

# Buttered Brazils

*These are very useful for decorating cakes and special puddings. You can also make buttered almonds and pine nuts by following the same method.*

1 oz (25 g) powdered glucose
¼ pint (150 ml) water
8 oz (225 g) granulated sugar

1 oz (25 g) butter
just under 4 oz (100 g) shelled
  Brazil nuts

Put the glucose, water and sugar into a heavy pan and leave over a low heat until the sugar has completely dissolved; do not allow the mixture to boil at this stage.

When the sugar has dissolved, boil the syrup to 'crack' (310 °F, 154 °C). If you do not have a sugar thermometer, boil the syrup until it is golden brown. Beat in the butter, then drop in the nuts, making sure that they are thoroughly coated with toffee.

Lightly oil a baking sheet and spoon on the nuts and leave them to set. Do not reboil any syrup left in the pan as it will go cloudy.

When the Buttered Brazils are hard they may be wrapped, if liked. Store in an airtight tin.

# Cashew Nut

Kidney-shaped, with a bland, sweet flavour, the cashew is sold without a shell and is among the more expensive of the nuts. India is one of the major exporting countries. It is not eaten raw, but lightly roasted to remove the remains of the acid liquid which surrounds the kernel in its shell.

The nuts can be bought whole or in pieces. They freeze well.

For recipe using cashew nuts, see:
Nut and Apple Roast, 182

# Chestnut

It is the sweet Spanish chestnut that we eat. The horse chestnut – the small boy's conker – is inedible. The shiny brown sweet chestnuts are encased in a prickly green outer husk that splits when the nut is ripe and is removed before it is sold. The nuts must be cooked and shelled before eating. Cut the shell right round with a sharp knife and boil for 20 to 30 minutes. The shell and the inner skin can then be peeled off, leaving the sweet-tasting nut.

Incidentally, the wise holidaymaker in Spain buys dried chestnuts in the local markets. The price there is very reasonable and a supply will keep for a year in a cool larder. Ready shelled, they can be soaked overnight and used as raw chestnuts.

The season in Britain is from October to December.

Use chestnuts in stuffing for the Christmas turkey, chopped with Brussels sprouts or other vegetables. Or just roast them by the fire on a winter night until the shell splits to release the mealy sweet nut. Try not to burn your fingers!

You can buy puréed chestnuts for cooking. And there are the French ones – *marrons* – that come canned or preserved. These are the basis of the famous *marrons glacés* and some *very* rich sweets.

Chestnuts can be frozen. First remove every bit of skin. Blanch for one to two minutes and then plunge them into cold water. When cold, pack them in strong polythene bags.

# Coconut

These fruits are large nuts with a hard, dark-brown outer shell closely covered with coarse fibres. The flesh is firm and white and, when young, the nuts contain a clear sweet liquid called coconut milk. To test a whole coconut for freshness, shake it and listen for the sound of the liquid inside.

At the top of the nut are three indentations or 'eyes'. Pierce two of these with a sharp nail and a hammer and pour out the milk, which can be chilled to make a pleasant drink. Then put the coconut, eyes down, on a hard surface and hit it with the hammer. The shell should split open and the flesh can be scooped out with a curved grapefruit knife.

Coconut can be bought dried or desiccated from delicatessens. Use desiccated coconut in cakes and puddings, or biscuits. Or you can delight the children by making coconut ice.

The flesh of the coconut keeps well in the refrigerator.

# Filbert

Filberts are the cultivated version of hazel or cob nuts. Hazel or cob nuts are round, smooth and, when picked from the tree, partly covered by leafy husks. Filberts are flask-shaped and wholly covered by their husks.

Look for ripe, fresh nuts. They can be bought with or without husks, but, for cooking, to buy them without saves time and energy.

Use filberts as dessert nuts or chopped in cakes or to coat a cold soufflé. Ground hazelnuts can be added to a meringue or pavlova, or to a whisked sponge mixture – substitute 1 oz (25 g) ground hazelnuts for the same quantity of flour. They can be ground in a blender, a few at a time.

Filberts freeze well.

Recipe:

## Hazelnut Biscuits

Makes 24 biscuits

*Hazelnuts have a very strong and distinctive flavour and there is never any need to use a large quantity. Almonds could also be used.*

2 oz (50 g) hazelnuts
4 oz (100 g) butter, softened
3 oz (75 g) light soft brown sugar

6 oz (175 g) plain flour
a little sieved icing sugar

Heat the oven to 350 °F, 180 °C, gas mark 4.

Lightly toast the hazelnuts under a moderate grill, then place them in a clean tea towel and rub in order to remove all the skins. Put 24 whole nuts on one side and then put the remainder in a blender and run until finely chopped. If you do not have a blender, chop very finely on a board.

Cream the butter and sugar together until they are fluffy, then gradually work in the flour and the ground nuts to make a firm dough.

Roll out on a lightly floured surface to about $\frac{1}{8}$ inch (3 mm) thick and, using a plain cutter, cut out 24 biscuits. Carefully lift these on to 2 or 3 lightly greased baking sheets. Place 1 whole hazelnut on top of each biscuit and prick the surface with a fork.

Bake the biscuits in the oven for 15 to 20 minutes until firm. Carefully lift them off and leave to cool on a wire rack.

Dust with icing sugar before serving.

# Peanut

Besides being the name of a well-known strip cartoon, peanuts are also called monkey nuts. They are the ground nuts that go into margarine, and, obviously, they can be turned into peanut butter.

Peanuts come in a curved, beige-coloured shell which can be easily broken with the fingers. Each shell contains a few small oval-shaped nuts covered with a red brown skin. They are at their best nibbled with pre-dinner drinks, and for this purpose you can buy them without their skins, roasted and salted. You can use peanuts in any recipe that specifies almonds – this gives a different flavour but peanuts are cheaper! They are also good in salads and rice dishes and to serve as a side dish with a curry.

Store peanuts in an airtight container, or freeze.

**Recipe:**
Nut and Apple Roast, 182

For other recipes using peanuts,
see Almond

**Recipe also using peanuts:**
Golden Walnut Cutlets, 184

# Nut and Apple Roast

Serves 4

*This is a very nutritious nut loaf. It does not look very exciting when you turn it out of the tin, so do decorate it with more nuts, tomato and parsley. It freezes well.*

| | |
|---|---|
| 4 oz (100 g) dry roasted peanuts | 1 oz (25 g) rolled oats |
| 4 oz (100 g) shelled cashew nuts | 1 level teaspoon mixed herbs |
| 2 oz (50 g) butter | salt |
| 1 large onion, chopped | ground black pepper |
| 1 large tomato, skinned and chopped | 1 egg, beaten |
| | a little milk |
| 2 small dessert apples, peeled, cored and diced | sliced tomato and parsley to garnish |

Heat the oven to 350 °F, 180 °C, gas mark 4. Grease a 1 lb (450 g) loaf tin.

Finely chop the nuts, reserving 8 whole cashew nuts for garnish. Heat the butter in a saucepan. Add the onion, tomato and apple and fry for about 5 minutes or until soft. Add the nuts, oats, herbs and seasoning to taste; take care when adding the salt as the nuts may be salty. Bind with the beaten egg and just enough milk to make a fairly moist consistency.

Press the mixture into the loaf tin and cover with a piece of lightly greased foil. Bake in the oven for about 1 hour until firm. Remove the foil for the last 15 minutes of the cooking time.

Turn out on to a warm serving dish, garnish with the whole cashew nuts, sliced tomato and parsley.

Serve either hot or cold with a green salad or with a vegetable.

# Pecan Nut

The pecan nut has a smooth, red-brown, shiny shell. The kernels look rather like elongated walnuts, but they are fleshier and have thinner shells and so can be cracked more easily. Look for dry, smooth nuts which are shiny and feel heavy. They may be bought dry and should be crisp yet moist and smooth to eat. They add an American dash to pies and salads.

Keep them dry in an airtight container in a cool dry place, or store them in the freezer if you prefer.

For recipe using pecan nuts, see:
American Walnut Pie, 188

# Pine Nut

Pine kernels, or pignolias, are the seeds of a variety of pine tree. Always sold without their shells, they are cylindrical in shape, creamy-coloured with a soft, oily texture and they have a delicious flavour if they are toasted or fried and salted. Pine nuts are very good in stuffings or fried in butter and oil and then scattered over sole or trout. They are rather pretty and look good in salads. Pine nuts tend to be rather expensive and perhaps should be kept for special occasions only.

Choose nuts that are crisp, dry and a bright cream colour. Store them in an airtight container or in the freezer.

For recipes using pine nuts, see:
Buttered Brazils, 177

Treacle and Fresh Walnut Tart, 185

Walnut Fudge, 186

# Walnut

Walnut trees grow well in the south of England but the nuts rarely ripen fully.

Dried walnuts for dessert are imported, mostly around Christmas time. The rounded brown shells should have a faint sheen. The shell cracks neatly into two parts to reveal the twisted, curly-shaped nut. You can also buy the nuts shelled, whole or chopped, for cooking. Keep them in an airtight container in a cool place. Use them for flavouring and decorating cakes, puddings and biscuits.

Freeze walnuts, in or out of the shell, in strong polythene bags.

## Golden Walnut Cutlets

Serves 2

*These cutlets have a very interesting texture and are not too expensive to make. They make an excellent vegetarian meal.*

1 small onion, finely chopped
1 tablespoon oil
4 oz (100 g) walnuts and
    peanuts mixed, chopped
1½ oz (40 g) rolled oats

1 egg, beaten
2 tablespoons milk
salt and pepper
oil for frying

Fry the onion in the oil for about 5 minutes, until it is soft, then stir in the nuts and oats and mix well. Add the beaten egg and milk and season well. Divide the mixture into two and shape each like a meat cutlet.

Heat a little oil in a frying pan and fry the cutlets over a moderate heat for about 3 minutes on each side until they are brown and crisp.

Serve with a hot green vegetable.

# Treacle and Fresh Walnut Tart                    Serves 8

*For a change you can try this recipe with pine nuts.*

6 oz (175 g) plain flour
1½ oz (40 g) margarine
1½ oz (40 g) lard
about 6 teaspoons cold water
   to mix
about 9 lightly rounded
   tablespoons golden syrup

about 9 tablespoons fresh white
   breadcrumbs
grated rind and juice of half a
   lemon
2 oz (50 g) walnuts, chopped

Put the flour in a bowl, add the fats, cut into small pieces, and rub in with the fingertips until the mixture resembles fine breadcrumbs. Add sufficient cold water to mix to a firm dough. Roll out on a floured surface and line a 9 inch (22.5 cm) deep flan or sandwich tin. Leave in the refrigerator while preparing the filling.

Heat the oven to 400 °F, 200 °C, gas mark 6.

Warm the syrup in a saucepan until it is runny and then stir in the breadcrumbs. Leave to stand for 10 minutes or until the crumbs have absorbed the syrup, then stir in the lemon rind and juice. Because it is difficult to be accurate when measuring golden syrup, add a little more syrup if the mixture looks too thick, or more breadcrumbs if it appears to be a little runny.

Add the walnuts and pour the filling into the pastry case. Bake in the oven for 10 minutes, reduce the heat to 375 °F, 190 °C, gas mark 5 and bake for a further 15 minutes or until the tart is cooked. Leave to cool in the tin for a short time and then serve warm, with cream.

# Baclava

Serves 8

*Baclava is a delicious, very sweet, Greek dessert. Phyllo pastry is quite widely available and can be found in delicatessens and continental food shops.*

8 oz (225 g) phyllo pastry (also called filo or fillo)

4 oz (100 g) unsalted butter, melted

4 oz (100 g) walnuts, chopped fairly finely

1 oz (25 g) caster sugar

thin honey

Heat the oven to 400°F, 200°C, gas mark 6. Butter a Swiss roll tin measuring 11 by 7 inches (27.5 by 17.5 cm).

Cut the pastry in half so that it is roughly the size of the tin. Lay one sheet of pastry in the tin, brush with butter and continue until there are eight layers in the tin. Brush the top layer with butter and sprinkle with nuts and sugar.

Finish with a further eight layers of pastry, brushing with butter between the layers. Brush the top with more butter and then cut through to the tin in diamond shapes.

Bake for 25 to 30 minutes until the baclava is pale golden brown and crispy. Cool in the tin.

Heat a little honey in a small saucepan and then brush it over the baclava to give a good glaze.

# Walnut Fudge

Makes 36 pieces

*Fudge makes a good present – delicious to eat and inexpensive to make. Instead of walnuts you can use chopped hazelnuts or chopped pine nuts.*

6 oz (196 g) can evaporated milk

3 oz (75 g) butter

1 lb (450 g) granulated sugar

¼ pint (150 ml) water

¼ teaspoon vanilla essence

2 oz (50 g) walnuts, chopped

Butter a shallow 7 inch (17.5 cm) square tin.

Put the evaporated milk, butter, sugar and water into a heavy pan and heat slowly, without boiling, until the sugar has dissolved. Then boil, steadily, stirring constantly, to 237 °F, 114 °C, or until a small amount of the mixture forms a soft ball when dropped into a glass of water. If the water becomes cloudy and the mixture dissolves, then the fudge is not yet ready.

Remove the pan from the heat and add the vanilla essence and walnuts. Cool slightly and then beat until the mixture thickens and begins to crystallise on the spoon.

Pour into the tin and leave to set. When firm cut into 36 squares and store in an airtight tin.

# Walnut Gingers                  Makes about 48 biscuits

*The children enjoy helping to roll out these cookies, but to save time you can put the mixture into a 7 by 11 inch (17.5 by 27.5 cm) tin and, when cooked, cut it into squares.*

4 oz (100 g) butter  
2 tablespoons golden syrup  
12 oz (350 g) self-raising flour  
2 level teaspoons ground ginger  
1 level teaspoon bicarbonate of  
  soda  

8 oz (225 g) granulated sugar  
2 oz (50 g) walnuts, finely  
  chopped  
1 egg, beaten  

Heat the oven to 300 °F, 150 °C, gas mark 2. Well grease several baking sheets.

Melt the butter and syrup in a saucepan. Sieve the flour, ginger and bicarbonate of soda into a bowl and stir in the sugar and walnuts. Pour in the melted butter and syrup and the beaten egg and mix well together with a fork, finishing with the hands, until the mixture is smooth and leaves the sides of the bowl clean.

Divide the mixture into small balls, each the size of a walnut, and place these on the baking sheets, leaving room for the biscuits to spread.

Bake the biscuits in the oven for 10 to 15 minutes until they are a light golden brown. Remove them from the oven and leave to cool on the baking sheet for 2 to 3 minutes, then lift off and leave to cool on a wire rack. Store in an airtight tin.

# American Walnut Pie

Serves 6

*This recipe derives from the classic pecan pie of the southern states of America, and you can use pecans instead of walnuts if you like. It tastes incredibly sweet.*

**Pastry:**
4 oz (100 g) plain flour
2 oz (50 g) butter
1 oz (25 g) lard
1 egg yolk
½ oz (12.5 g) caster sugar
1 teaspoon water

**Filling:**
1 oz (25 g) butter
6 oz (175 g) light soft brown sugar
3 eggs
8 oz (227 g) jar maple syrup
1 teaspoon vanilla essence
¼ teaspoon salt
3 oz (75 g) walnuts

First make the pastry: put the flour in a bowl, add the fats, cut into small pieces, and rub them in with the fingertips until the mixture resembles fine breadcrumbs. Mix the egg yolk with the sugar and water and stir into the dry ingredients to bind them together.

Wrap the pastry in cling film and chill in the refrigerator for 30 minutes.

Heat the oven to 425 °F, 220 °C, gas mark 7.

Roll out the pastry on a floured surface and line an 8 inch (20 cm) loose-bottomed deep flan tin. Line the flan with greaseproof paper, weigh down with baking beans and bake blind for 10 minutes. Remove the paper and beans and return the flan to the oven for a further 5 minutes to dry out the base.

To make the filling: cream the butter and sugar together, whisk the eggs and add them to the creamed mixture with the maple syrup, vanilla essence and salt. Beat well.

Arrange the walnuts over the base of the flan, flat side down. Pour in the filling. Reduce the oven temperature to 375 °F, 190 °C, gas mark 5, and bake for about 40 minutes. The pie will rise and fall back on cooling.

Serve warm with cream.

# Pickled Walnuts

*Walnuts should be pickled while they are still green and under ripe, before the shells have begun to form. If you do pickle your own, look out – walnut juice can stain your skin dark brown.*

*Whole spices are preferred for spicing vinegar. For soft pickles, such as walnuts, use hot vinegar. Cold spiced vinegar is best for pickling vegetables, such as cabbage or onion, which should be kept crisp.*

walnuts
salt
water

*Spiced vinegar:*
2 pints (1 litre) malt vinegar
¼ oz (6.5 g) cinnamon bark
¼ oz (6.5 g) cloves
¼ oz (6.5 g) mace
¼ oz (6.5 g) whole allspice
a few peppercorns or a pinch of
    cayenne pepper

Cover the walnuts with a brine made of 1 lb (450 g) salt to 1 gallon (4.5 litres) water and soak for several days, then change the brine and soak the nuts for a further week.

Drain, spread the walnuts on trays and expose them to the air until they turn black – this will take about 24 hours.

To make spiced vinegar, place vinegar and spices in a basin, cover with a plate and place in a saucepan of water. Bring the water to the boil and then remove the saucepan from the heat. Allow the spices to steep in the warm vinegar for 2 hours. Strain the vinegar and use.

Pack the walnuts into jars and cover well with spiced vinegar. Cover and seal. Leave them for at least a month before use.

# Miscellaneous Recipes

## Basic Ice Cream

*This is one of the simplest and best ice creams.*

4 eggs, separated
4 oz (100 g) caster sugar

½ pint (300 ml) double cream

Whisk the yolks in a small bowl until they are blended. In a larger bowl, whisk the egg whites until they are stiff, then whisk in the sugar, a teaspoonful at a time; the whites will get stiffer and stiffer as the sugar is added.

Whisk the cream until it forms soft peaks and then fold it, with the egg yolks, into the meringue mixture.

Turn the ice cream into a 2½ pint (1.4 litre) container. Cover, label and freeze.

Leave to thaw at room temperature for 5 minutes, then serve scoops in small glasses or dishes.

## Flavourings to add to the basic ice cream

### Apricot

Take 8 oz (225 g) stoned apricots and put them in a saucepan with 3 tablespoons water and 2 oz (50 g) caster sugar. Cook very slowly until the fruit is quite soft and tender. Purée in a blender until smooth. Leave to become quite cold and then fold into the basic ice cream just before freezing.

### Blackberry

Take 8 to 12 oz (225 to 350 g) fresh blackberries and put in a blender with 1 to 2 oz (25 to 50 g) icing sugar and purée until smooth. Sieve to remove pips and then stir into the basic ice cream just before freezing.

## Black currant

Make as for apricot purée, sieve, cool and then fold into the ice cream just before freezing.

## Gooseberry

Top and tail 8 oz (225 g) gooseberries and make a purée as for apricots, then pass through a sieve to remove all the pips; if you have puréed the fruit first this stage is very easy. Leave to become quite cold and then fold into the basic ice cream just before freezing.

## Loganberry

Make as for Blackberry Ice Cream.

## Melon

Remove the seeds from half an Ogen or galia melon. Scoop out the flesh from the shell and purée it in the blender with the juice of 2 lemons. Turn into a container and freeze until mushy. Make the basic ice cream and fold in the partially frozen melon purée and freeze as usual.

## Mint and Lemon

Whisk the double cream with grated rind and juice of 2 lemons until it forms soft peaks, then fold it, with a handful of finely chopped mint, into the meringue.

## Mulberry

Make as for Blackberry Ice cream.

## Peach

Take 4 large yellow peaches, peel, quarter them and remove the stones. Put the flesh in the blender, together with 1 oz (25 g) icing sugar and run until a smooth purée. Stir into the basic ice cream just before freezing; if liked add a few drops of yellow colouring.

### Pineapple

Cut the flesh from a small pineapple, add the juice of a small lemon and 2 oz (50 g) icing sugar and purée in a blender. Put into a container and freeze until just set. Fold into the basic ice cream just before freezing.

### Raspberry

Make as for Blackberry Ice Cream.

### Strawberry

Hull 8 to 12 oz (225 g to 350 g) fresh strawberries and make a purée as for Blackberry Ice Cream. Stir into the basic ice cream just before freezing.

# Fruit Syrup

½ pint (300 ml) water         juice of 1 lemon
8 oz (225 g) granulated sugar     few sprigs mint

Put the water and sugar in a saucepan and heat slightly until the sugar has dissolved. Bring to the boil, then take off the heat. Add the lemon juice and mint and leave to cool.

Use to sweeten fruit and for fruit salads etc.

# Index

# Index

# A–Z OF
# HOME
# FREEZING
## Mary Norwak

Can eggs be frozen in their shells? How do avocados react to cold storage? Is there any point in freezing herbs? In over 500 detailed entries, the *A–Z of Home Freezing* answers every question freezer-owners might want to ask – from what to freeze, how to freeze and when to freeze, to deep freeze installation, running costs, wrapping, labelling, de-freezing and re-freezing. In addition to the A–Z section and a complete index for easy reference, there is a special monthly calendar of deep-freezing recipes.

COOKERY     0 7221 6463 7     £1·75

# Rosalie Swedlin

# WORLD OF SALADS

Rosalie Swedlin, an American by birth and bred on salads, has lived in London for many years. Having worked in publishing she has a full appreciation of the necessity to make cookery books practical, readable and fun to use and this, her first cookery book, is exactly that. WORLD OF SALADS is designed both for the beginner and for the experienced cook to introduce them to new tastes and ingredients from round the world, and to act as a starting point and inspiration so that people everywhere can explore the creativity and endless variety of salads.

COOKERY   0 7221 8310 0   £2.75

# A SELECTION OF BESTSELLERS FROM *SPHERE*

**FICTION**

| | | |
|---|---|---|
| A PERFECT STRANGER | Danielle Steel | £1.75 ☐ |
| MISSING PERSONS | C. Terry Cline Jr | £1.95 ☐ |
| A GREEN DESIRE | Anton Myrer | £2.50 ☐ |
| FLOODTIDE | Suzanne Goodwin | £1.95 ☐ |
| JADE TIGER | Craig Thomas | £2.25 ☐ |

**FILM & TV TIE-INS**

| | | |
|---|---|---|
| THE YEAR OF LIVING DANGEROUSLY | C. J. Koch | £1.75 ☐ |
| STAR WARS | George Lucas | £1.75 ☐ |
| FAME | Leonore Fleischer | £1.75 ☐ |
| UPSTAIRS, DOWNSTAIRS | John Hawkesworth | £1.50 ☐ |

**NON-FICTION**

| | | |
|---|---|---|
| A QUESTION OF BALANCE | H.R.H. The Duke of Edinburgh | £1.50 ☐ |
| THE DEATH OF THE DIAMOND | Edward Jay Epstein | £1.95 ☐ |
| SUSAN'S STORY | Susan Hampshire | £1.75 ☐ |
| SECOND LIFE | Stephani Cook | £1.95 ☐ |
| YOU CAN TEACH YOUR CHILD INTELLIGENCE | David Lewis | £1.95 ☐ |

*All Sphere books are available at your local bookshop or newsagent, or can be ordered direct from the publisher. Just tick the titles you want and fill in the form below.*

Name _____

Address _____

_____

Write to Sphere Books, Cash Sales Department, P.O. Box 11, Falmouth, Cornwall TR10 9EN.

Please enclose cheque or postal order to the value of the cover price plus:

UK: 45p for the first book, 20p for the second and 14p per copy for each additional book ordered to a maximum charge of £1.63.

OVERSEAS: 75p for the first book and 21p for each additional book.

BFPO & EIRE: 45p for the first book, 20p for the second book plus 14p per copy for the next 7 books, thereafter 8p per book.

*Sphere Books reserve the right to show new retail prices on covers which may differ from those previously advertised in the text or elsewhere, and to increase postal rates in accordance with the PO.*